George Washington

1st President of
the United States

A portrait of Washington painted in 1796 by the noted American artist, Gilbert Stuart. (Library of Congress.)

George Washington

1st President of the United States

Lucille Falkof

GARRETT EDUCATIONAL CORPORATION

Copyright © 1989 by Lucille Falkof
All rights reserved including the right of reproduction in whole or in part in any form without the prior written permission of the publisher. Published by Garrett Educational Corporation, 130 East 13th Street, P.O. Box 1588, Ada, Oklahoma 74820.

Manufactured in the United States of America

Edited and produced by Synthegraphics Corporation

Library of Congress Cataloging in Publication Data

Falkof, Lucille, 1924–
  George Washington, 1st president of the United States.

  (Presidents of the United States)
  Bibliography: p.
  Includes index.
  Summary: Follows the life of George Washington, including his childhood, education, employment, political career, and term of presidency.
  1. Washington, George, 1732–1799—Juvenile literature. 2. Presidents—United States—Biography—Juvenile literature. [1. Washington, George, 1732–1799. 2. Presidents.] I. Title. II. Title: George Washington, first president of the United States. III. Series.
  E312.66.F34 1989 973.4'1'0924—dc19 [B] [92]
  88-24564
  ISBN 0-944483-19-4

Contents

Chronology for
George Washington

1732   Born on February 22

1749   Commissioned as a surveyor

1753   Sent by Governor Dinwiddie of Virginia
to deliver letter of warning to the
French in the Ohio Terrritory

1755- Served in the French and Indian War
1759

1759   Married Martha Custis on January 6;
became a member of the Virginia
House of Burgesses

1774   Attended First Continental Congress

1775   Appointed commander-in-chief of
American forces by the Continental
Congress

1776   Forced evacuation of British from Boston

1781   Defeated Cornwallis at Battle of
Yorktown

1783   Retired from military service

1787   Elected President of Constitutional
Convention

1789   Unanimously elected first President of the
United States

1793   Unanimously re-elected for second term
as President

1799   Died on December 14

Chapter 1
The Great Betrayal

Betrayed! The hand holding the sheaf of papers trembled with rage. "Arnold has turned traitor!" The words dropped bitterly from George Washington's lips. "He has betrayed us to the British!" Rarely did the general show his emotions. His young aide, red-headed Alexander Hamilton, had never seen Washington so upset.

The day had started so well. The trees along the route to West Point, New York, had vied with each other in showing off their brilliant fall foliage. The crisp September air had invigorated Washington's spirits. He had been looking forward to the reunion with his old friend, Benedict Arnold, the commanding general at West Point. They were to discuss the plans for reinforcing the fort.

After five years of war, the news during the summer of 1780 had been very depressing. The Americans had been defeated twice in South Carolina, once at Camden and again at Charleston. If the American Revolution was ever to succeed, the Continental Army needed more victories of the kind Arnold had achieved at the Battle of Saratoga in October 1777.

FROM HERO TO TRAITOR

General Arnold was a superb soldier with a brilliant war record. It was a shame that his efforts had not always been appreciated. He had fought valiantly at Saratoga and, during the course of the battle, had been badly crippled by a leg wound. Washington felt that Arnold deserved a relatively easy assignment after Saratoga, one that would help him to rest and regain his health. So when the British, under General Henry Clinton, evacuated Philadelphia, Washington had appointed Arnold as military commander of the city. He also hoped it would, in some measure, repay Arnold for the fact that he had been denied a well-earned promotion.

Unfortunately, Arnold had not been in Philadelphia long when rumors began to circulate that he was using his position to make money for himself. Not only was he living in grand style, he was also courting a beautiful and well-born young woman, Peggy Shippen, whom he later married. The fact that she was a Tory, an American still loyal to the British crown, compounded the situation.

For months, the Continental Congress investigated Arnold's financial affairs in Philadelphia and his relationship with Peggy Shippen. During this time, Washington was torn between sympathy and affection for Arnold and the need for Congress to handle the investigation without his interference. Washington had heaved a sigh of relief when Arnold was declared innocent of the charges.

Following his acquittal, Arnold requested assignment to West Point. How could Washington have known what was in Arnold's mind when he asked for command of the fortress at West Point—the key to the Hudson River Valley and New York City?

Washington had sent word ahead that he hoped to dine with Arnold and his bride in the early afternoon. On arrival, he was told that Peggy Arnold was asleep and that General Arnold was not available but would join them later for dinner. Washington thought it was strange that there were so few men in attendance and that Arnold was not immediately available to the Commander-in-Chief. Nevertheless, he proceeded to inspect the fort and was appalled to find how much repair work had to be done. Certainly Arnold and his 1,800 men had a large task ahead of them.

Washington had been freshening up for the evening meal when Hamilton had interrupted with the sheaf of papers. Now in control of his emotions, Washington sank into a chair and looked through the packet of papers again.

A Tale of Treachery

Turning to Hamilton, Washington said, "These papers were taken from a British officer, Major John Andre, who is an aide to General Clinton. Our soldiers stopped Andre as he was trying to get through the American lines, disguised as a man named John Anderson. He carried a pass signed by General Arnold. Hidden in his stockings were these papers, which contain information about the army's strength at West Point and plans for the defense of the fort—all in Arnold's handwriting! There is no doubt that General Arnold planned to turn over West Point to the British."

For a moment, Washington paused and shook his head. Then he went on. "I can't believe this! Why, there is even a copy of the minutes of a council of war I held on September 6. This packet also contains a letter from Andre addressed to me. In it, he confesses that he met with Arnold to discuss the final details of the plot and that he was seized while racing back to General Clinton with the plans."

Hamilton looked at Washington's weary face. "But how did Arnold learn about the capture of Andre?"

"Simple," answered Washington. "The officer who captured Andre did not know Arnold was in on the plot and did what any officer should do—he reported the incident to his commanding officer, who, in this case, was General Arnold. As soon as Arnold realized that his plans had been discovered, he fled. One of Arnold's officers told me that Arnold had received a message this morning while eating breakfast. He seemed very upset and left the table shortly after. That must have been the message from the officer who captured Andre."

Suddenly Washington remembered that Peggy Arnold was supposed to be upstairs in bed. Checking with an aide, he learned that the young woman was still in her room, crying hysterically. Washington then went upstairs to question her concerning Arnold's whereabouts, but his efforts proved futile. Each time he asked her a question about her husband's escape route, Mrs. Arnold would only sob louder. Finally, there was nothing Washington could do but agree to her request to be sent back to her family in Philadelphia. (Later, he would learn that it was Mrs. Arnold who had arranged the first introduction of Major Andre to General Arnold.)

Hamilton was dispatched immediately to try and capture Arnold before he was safely behind enemy lines. Arnold, however, succeeded in escaping and was later rewarded with a commission as brigadier general in the British Army.

Why had Arnold defected to the enemy? Was he angry at his treatment by the Continental Congress? Did he feel his efforts as an officer were not appreciated? Or was it to please his young and beautiful Tory wife?

After the story of Arnold's treachery made every newspaper in the colonies, he was hanged in effigy in Philadelphia, Boston, and other towns. To the American public, he became a symbol of betrayal. To call someone a "Benedict Arnold" was to call him a traitor.

The affair was a difficult one for Washington. He felt personally betrayed because of all his efforts on Arnold's behalf. Both as Commander-in-Chief of the Continental Army and as first President of the United States, Washington would later suffer other incidents when his personal feelings and his reputation would be affected. But as always, he would handle them with dignity and a determination to do what was best for the country.

Chapter 2

Everyone Needs Heroes

George Washington came from a family that prized land. The Washington men were not only willing to work hard to attain their goals, they also realized that it helped to marry into families where their brides provided rich doweries of land.

It was in 1657, just 50 years after the settlement of Jamestown, Virginia, that John Washington, George's great-grandfather, arrived in the colony of Virginia. He had come to America as a mate on a ship that ran aground as it was returning to England with a cargo of tobacco. While waiting for the ship to be repaired, John found time to court and marry the daughter of a wealthy planter. With his wife's dowry of 700 acres of land, the young couple established their roots in America and prospered.

Under Augustine Washington, who was John's grandson and George's father, the original 700 acres of land became a 2,500-acre estate, called Epsewasson, in Westmoreland County, Virginia. Augustine also owned a mill and was a partner in an iron works in England. In 1729, upon returning from a business trip to England, he discovered that his wife had died, leaving him with three children: Lawrence, Augustine, Jr., and Jane. Needing to find a mother for his children, Augustine married a woman named Mary Ball in 1731. She was from a well-to-do family and brought a dowry of 400 acres to her new family.

At ages 12 and 13, respectively, the two boys, Augustine, Jr., and Lawrence, were sent to school in England while nine-year-old Jane stayed at home with her new stepmother. She did not remain an only child for long, however. On February 22nd, 1732, Mary gave birth to her first child, a boy whom she and Augustine named George.

A COLONIAL EDUCATION

In 1735 young George suffered his first loss, the death of his half-sister, Jane. This was also the year when Augustine moved his family from their home at Epsewasson to Ferry Farm, a piece of land that he owned along the Rappahannock River, across from Fredericksburg, Virginia. It was at Ferry Farm that George began his schooling at age six, first learning to read and write and then to do arithmetic. Indeed, counting became George's passion, with a love of numbers and record-keeping that would remain with him all his life.

George enjoyed reading, but his taste tended to be more practical than poetic. As a young boy, he carefully read *The Young Man's Companion*, which listed rules on how to be a gentleman, how to measure land and lumber, and how to write letters to people of quality. (In later life, his library contained volumes with such titles as *Diseases of Horses* and *The Complete Farmer*.) Whatever formal education George had probably ended by the time he was 13 years old.

WASHINGTON'S FIRST HERO

In 1738 George's half-brother, Lawrence, completed his schooling in England and returned to Virginia. For a six-year-old boy, nothing could have been more exciting than to discover a big brother. Lawrence had manners, grace, and an elegant bearing. He was a man who preferred horses to books, yet he reasoned and wrote well and had a sharp political sense. Young George was captivated by his brother, and the feeling was mutual. When war broke out between Spain and England in 1739, Lawrence was named as one of the four leaders of the Virginia Company assigned to the British Navy and had to leave again. But the figure of Lawrence in the dazzling uniform of a naval officer convinced George that he, too, was meant for military life.

When George was 11 years old, his father died suddenly. Under Augustine's will, the family home at Epsewasson went to Lawrence, with the provision that it would go to George if Lawrence died without heirs. George was to receive Ferry Farm, as well as 10 slaves and three lots of land, when he came of age at 21. On the Epsewasson land, Lawrence built a typical two-story colonial home and renamed the estate Mount Vernon. He also married Anne Fairfax, a member of one of the most important and wealthiest families in Virginia.

Though George continued to live at Ferry Farm under the watchful eye of his mother, he began to spend more and more time at Mount Vernon. He loved the elegant society in which Lawrence and his wife moved, and he loved the stories that Lawrence told about the glories of military life. Much of the talk at Mount Vernon also centered around the new lands that were being opened in the western frontier of Virginia, for which Lawrence's father-in-law, Colonel William Fairfax, was responsible for the issuance of land grants. The more George heard, the more he aspired to own some of this land and the wealth it might bring him.

LIFE WITH MOTHER

When George was 14 years old, Lawrence suggested that George might have a promising career in the British Royal Navy. For this, George needed his mother's consent, but Mary Washington would not hear of it. She was determined to keep her oldest son close to her, away from the dangers of either the sea or the frontier.

The relationship between mother and son was not a happy one. All through his life, George made a real effort to be a dutiful and helpful son, but from his teen years on, relations with his mother were strained. Mary Washington was set in her ways and in her thinking. She could not manage money and constantly complained to those who would listen to her that she never had enough funds to meet her needs. Although George inherited Ferry Farm, his mother never offered to turn it over to him even though he was legally entitled to the property when he turned 21.

There are no stories from George's youth that describe warm and happy events between mother and son. Nor are there any letters that reflect that his mother took pride in George's achievements, though she lived until he was elected first President of the United States.

A Second Hero

Another opportunity to get out from under his mother's influence arose when George was 16 years old. As a result of having spent much time with Lawrence and Anne at Mount Vernon, he was now also included in the society at Belvoir, the beautiful estate of Anne's father, Colonel William Fairfax. It was at Belvoir that George met the colonel's oldest son, George William Fairfax, a polished young man who had been educated in England. Though only 23, the Fairfax heir was already a member of the Virginia legislature, called the House of Burgesses. The friendship bloomed when Fairfax and young George were asked to join a surveying party in the Shenandoah Valley.

A FIRST GLIMPSE OF THE FRONTIER

The task of the surveying party was to plot the Fairfax land in the Shenandoah Valley into farm size lots. Physically, George was well-prepared for the journey. He was over six feet tall and had the strength of a grown man. He also had surveying skills. Though he and young Fairfax were venturing out to the frontier, they did not travel as backwoodsmen. They carried watches rather than telling time by the sun, and instead of frontier clothing, they wore fashionable clothes of the day.

During the month-long journey, George gained first-hand knowledge about the Shenandoah Valley, the Indians who lived there, and the problems of the settlers. When he was commissioned as a surveyor in 1749, George used his first earnings to buy a tract of land in the valley.

TRAGEDY STRIKES

The years following 1749 were saddened by continuing tragedy in Lawrence Washington's home. Three of his children died and Lawrence himself developed a frightening and persistent cough. In 1751 George went with Lawrence to the island of Barbados, in the Caribbean, where they hoped that the fresh air and good climate would improve Lawrence's health. While on the trip, George became ill with smallpox. Although he recovered, the scars left by the illness remained all his life. But George knew that he now had a permanent immunity to the disease.

Upon his return home, George began to find time to socialize. He took dancing lessons and, for a large man with big hands and feet, proved to be quite adept. He also attempted several times to write sonnets to one or another of the young women he met. But he failed to make much headway with the ladies because he was too self-conscious and often found himself at a loss for words in their presence.

But nothing was as difficult for George to bear as the death of his beloved half-brother, Lawrence, at the age of 35. Having been George's mentor, model, and best friend, the loss was extremely painful to George. Lawrence bequeathed Mount Vernon to his remaining child, Sarah, with the provision that if she died without heirs, George would inherit the estate and all of Lawrence's property in Fairfax County. Sarah died two months later, and George became the owner of Mount Vernon.

Following Lawrence's death, George applied for Lawrence's position as an adjutant in the Virginia militia. The function of an adjutant was to "instruct the officers and soldiers in the use and exercise of their arms, in bringing the militia to a more regular discipline, and fitting it for service, besides polishing and improving the meaner people." Although he was not yet 21 and did not have any military training, George was appointed a major in the militia. He eventually learned what he needed to know about training officers and soldiers by reading manuals on military drill and regulations. George now had much to boast about: a military title, a profession, and more than 6,000 acres of land of his own.

Here, at Mount Vernon, his beloved home in Virginia, Washington entertained visitors from all over the world. (Library of Congress.)

Chapter 3
Learning from Necessity

Was it vanity, pride, arrogance, or a desire for adventure that led Washington to leave a prospering plantation life to carry a letter from the governor of Virginia, Robert Dinwiddie, 300 miles into the wilderness to the commander of a French fort? Whatever it was, Major Washington volunteered for the mission.

One of Lawrence Washington's business ventures had been to help organize the Ohio Company for the purpose of trading furs and developing land beyond the Allegheny Mountains. Unfortunately, the same lands were also claimed by the King of France. The British crown gave the Ohio Company 500,000 acres of land in the area, provided that the company built a fort and established 200 families there.

Although the French and British had been at war in Europe for many years, there was no open warfare between the two countries in America. Here on the new continent, both countries vied to make favorable treaties with the Indians and to establish forts on the Ohio River system.

GEORGE PLAYS POSTMAN

This was Washington's first assignment as an army officer, yet he appeared self-assured as he stood before Governor Dinwiddie to get his final instructions. "Major Washington," said Dinwiddie, "you have two missions to accomplish on this journey. First, you are to deliver this letter to the French commander at Fort LeBoeuf. It contains a warning to the French *not* to build forts or to settle in the area of the Ohio River system."

As George took the letter, Dinwiddie continued. "Your second assignment is to make friends with the Indians along the way. If war should break out, we will need them on our side." The governor then smiled as the 21-year-old Washington strode out, exuding confidence in every step.

Mission Accomplished

When Washington returned 2½ months later, he was wearing "an Indian walking dress": leather leggings, a knee-length coat belted at the waist, and moccasins. The outfit was markedly different from what he had worn on his surveying expedition with Fairfax, for he had learned the benefits of comfortable frontier garb. He had also gained self-assurance that he could cope under dangerous and demanding conditions, for he had been attacked by an Indian in ambush, had been forced to march over frozen terrain, and had nearly lost his life in the icy Allegheny River when his improvised raft had overturned while he was crossing the river.

When Washington met again with Dinwiddie in the Governor's Palace in Williamsburg, he was able to report that both missions had been accomplished. He had delivered the letter and carried back an answer from the French commander. He had also made contact with Half-King, one of the most powerful Indian chiefs in the territory. Half-King had assured Washington that his warriors would support the British. However, the Indian chief left Washington with words that so impressed him that he wrote them in his diary in capital letters: "TO COME, FATHERS, AND BUILD HOUSES UPON OUR LAND AND TO TAKE IT BY FORCE IS WHAT WE CANNOT SUBMIT TO."

It was clear that no matter what the French or English wanted, the Indians would not willingly give up their land to white settlers. Nor was the news about the French any better. Both the letter from the French commander and a report that Washington prepared left little doubt that the French were resolved to hold the Ohio River and its tributaries. From the more than 200 canoes that Washington saw at Fort LeBoeuf, he concluded that the French would soon be moving to enlarge their holdings in the Ohio territory.

When Governor Dinwiddie printed Washington's report of his mission, George learned for the first time the problems of being a public figure. Some of the men in Williamsburg, where the House of Burgesses met, applauded his report. On the other hand, Dinwiddie's enemies and some others accused Washington of magnifying the danger from the French.

FIRST BLOOD

Convinced that the English had to get to the Ohio River and begin building forts before the French did, Dinwiddie decided to send an expedition to the junction of the Monongahela and Allegheny rivers, at what is today Pittsburgh. Joshua Fry, a mathematics professor at William and Mary College, was given command of the party, though he had never served in any military capacity. Although George had neither the experience nor the age to command a company of 300 men, he was not bashful about speaking for himself to secure a role in the expedition or asking friends to recommend him to Dinwiddie. As a result, he became second in command, with the rank of lieutenant colonel. That was the easy part.

What was harder was recruiting men for the campaign. Though each colony had its own militia, this was to be a volunteer group, which meant that Fry and Washington had to do their own recruiting. They found few men willing to leave their families and farms to serve; those who did were "loose, idle men," lacking shoes and adequate clothing. With Fry remaining behind to continue recruitment, Washington set out with 150 raw soldiers. An advance party had been sent ahead to begin the building of the fort. Washington's task was to provide protection for these men.

The expedition had not advanced very far when Washington received the news that Fry had been killed by a fall from his horse. Not surprised by the news, Washington's only comment was, "He was too old and fat to move quickly anyway."

But even Washington, now the new commander, was having trouble moving quickly. Once past the small towns, Washington's troops advanced less than four miles a day, for his men had to hack a road through the wilderness as they went. It would turn out to be an important feat because, for the first time, the Ohio Valley would be open to wheeled vehicles and thus to settlement.

Bad News at Wills Creek

The news was grim! Arriving at Wills Creek in April 1754, Washington learned that the packhorses that had been ordered had not arrived and that he had only 12 wagons to transport supplies. Six days later, an Iroquois runner brought news that the French had swept down from the north with 1,000 men, 300 canoes, and eight cannon and destroyed the fort the English were building. The French were already beginning to build a new fort, called Fort DuQuesne.

Then came the final blow. Washington received word that the wages paid to officers, including himself, would be the same as those paid to volunteer foot soldiers. Dinwiddie had originally assured George that there would be a special pay scale for officers, equal to the pay of officers in the royal militia. Furious with this treatment, George vented his anger in a letter to Governor Dinwiddie:

> Giving up my commission is quite contrary to my intention. . . . But let me serve voluntarily; then I will, with the greatest pleasure in life, devote my services to the expedition, without any other reward than the satisfaction of serving my country; but to be slaving dangerously for the shadow of pay, through woods, rocks, mountains — I would rather prefer the great toil of a day laborer, and dig for maintenance . . . than serve on such ignoble terms; for I really do not see why the lives of his Majesty's subjects in Virginia should be of less value than those in other parts of his American dominion, especially when it is well known that we must undergo double their hardships. . . . I am determined not to leave the Regiment, but to be amongst the last men that quit the Ohio, even if I serve as a private volunteer, which I greatly prefer to the establishment we are now upon.

Offering to serve without a salary was a gesture Washington would make several times in his life, sometimes to his sorrow.

The Charming Whistle of Bullets

Without waiting for an answer to his letter, Washington marched his men to Great Meadows, Pennsylvania, and set up camp, believing the place would be "a charming field for an encounter." He would live to regret those words. On the morning of May 28, 1754, the backwoodsman who had guided him on his first mission to the French, arrived with the news that a French party was encamped not too far away. George was eager to strike first, to surprise the French.

The plan that George devised for the attack was one he would use several times during the early years of the Revolutionary War. With the help of Half-King and some of his warriors, Washington deployed several columns, with the Virginia troops advancing from the left and right and the Indians bringing up the rear.

The tactics worked. When the Indians and the Virginia soldiers were within 100 yards of the French camp, Washington gave the command to open fire. For 15 minutes the gunfire was heavy from both sides, then the French raised the white flag of surrender. But when the Indians rushed in to scalp the survivors, it was all Washington's men could do to prevent a massacre. Among those killed in the battle was the French commander.

Having experienced his first successful military action, George now felt more confident in his ability to lead men. However, he had not adhered strictly to his orders. George had not been ordered to attack the French. His orders were to counter any attack, and he had *assumed* the French meant to attack his small force. What had been a cold war had now turned into a hot one. What Washington considered merely his first encounter with war was, in fact, the opening of the French and Indian War.

Later in a letter to his brother John, George wrote, "I heard the bullets whistle, and believe me, there is something charming in the sound." The comment was reported in Williamsburg and in the British press. It was said that King George II, on hearing the words, commented that Washington would not consider the sound of bullets so charming "if he had been used to hear many." Later in life, when George was asked if it was true that he found charm in the whistle of bullets, he is reputed to have answered, "If I said so, it was when I was very young."

DEFEAT AT FORT NECESSITY

Returning to Great Meadows, Washington realized that he had better prepare for a retaliatory attack by the French. He had just begun to build a small fort, which he called Fort Necessity, when a group of Iroquois Indians arrived, mostly women and children, all expecting to be fed from the fort's meager food supplies. In addition, an independent company of 100 soldiers, led by a Captain James Mackay, had arrived. This presented another sticky problem for Washington. Who was in command—a colonel (George himself) who had been authorized by a colonial governor, or a captain who held his rank by order of King George II? It took nerve for George, who had just won his first battle, to debate the issue of command with an army officer who had 18 years of experience in Indian warfare. Though both men respected each other, neither George nor Mackay would agree to serve as second in command.

Before the issue of command could be resolved, an Indian arrived with word that more than 1,200 French and Indians were marching toward Great Meadows. Looking at the small fort, Washington no longer believed it to be a "charming field for an encounter." As the troops began to dig trenches in preparation for the coming battle, they discovered that the land was marshy. In addition, high ground surrounded the field—ground from which the enemy could attack.

On July 3 it began to rain, and it rained steadily for five hours. Suddenly, the sound of Indian war whoops and gunfire pierced the air. Washington ordered his soldiers into the open to repel the attack. The French were too far away for their first bullets to do any harm. But as they pressed closer, Washington ordered his men back into the trenches, which were now filled with water.

As Washington wrote later, "From every little rising, tree, stump, stone and bush [they] kept up a constant, galling fire upon us." Not only were men dying, but the enemy carefully picked off every horse and cow so that at the end, Washington's men had lost both their food and transportation. It was now almost impossible to keep the ammunition dry because the trenches were filled with a mixture of blood and water. Young, inexperienced, and flush from his first victory, George found it hard to think of surrendering.

Signing a Treacherous Surrender Document

As darkness fell, the enemy guns stopped. In the eerie silence, a voice called out, "*Voulez-vous parler?*" ("Do you want to talk?") Washington looked at the wounded and dying men and animals all around him. Without food and transportation, there was no way out. Mackay's and George's men had fought bravely against great odds, but they had no alternative except to surrender. When papers were offered, George courteously allowed Mackay to sign first. Whether it was the darkness or an inaccurate translation from the French, Washington failed to take notice of the following statement in the surrender papers offered by the French:

> Our intention has never been to trouble the peace and good harmony which reigns between two friendly princes, but only to avenge the assassination which has been done to one of our officers, the bearer of a summons.

The "assassination" referred to the death of the French

commander during Washington's first skirmish at Great Meadows. The incident soon became known as the Jumonville Affair, after the name of the French commander who had been killed, and was reported by the French as the assassination of an innocent officer who had come on a mission of peace. It was to make Washington an international figure and cause much damage to his reputation.

The terms of surrender were lenient and on July 4, 1754, to the solemn beat of drummers, Washington's ragged band of wounded and exhausted soldiers proceeded homeward.

Loss of Face

The battle at Fort Necessity had many repercussions. Washington's surrender made him lose face with the Indians. As one Indian agent said, "There were never the like seen how quick the nations turned after Colonel Washington's defeat." The Indians, now allied with the French, would harrass settlers on the frontier and later oppose the British Army under General Braddock.

In addition, the death of Jumonville was deemed by the French to be an assassination because there was no proof that the French advance had been intended to be anything other than a peaceful overture to the British. It gave the French the right to blame the war on Washington's impetuous behavior. English officers saw in Washington's two encounters with the enemy more bravery than good judgment.

In defense of his actions, George could blame the lack of supplies and the failure of adequate troops to arrive on time. He could also point to the problems of rank and command between royal and colonial commissioned officers. But the colonists who read about his exploits and his courage against superior numbers saw in Washington a brave and adventuresome hero.

Washington Resigns

Returning to Williamsburg, Washington learned that Governor Dinwiddie had a new plan to raise troops for the defense of the Ohio frontier. The Virginia regiment was to be broken up into independent companies. Washington would no longer be a colonel, but a captain, and not even one with a royal commission. Washington's pride was hurt, and he was indignant that his efforts had been so poorly rewarded. Despite efforts by friends to change his mind, Washington sent his resignation to Dinwiddie, and the governor accepted it. However, George did leave the door open for the future. In writing to friends, he asked that they convey to the governor the following, "Assure him . . . of my reluctance to quit the service and of the pleasure I should have received in attending his fortune. Also inform him that it was to obey the call of honor . . . I declined it, and not to gratify any desire I have to leave the military line."

Washington had closed the door, but it was not slammed shut.

Chapter 4

Lessons in Politics and War

There is nothing like practical experience to teach and to mold a man's character. George had learned from his wrangle over the royal versus the colonial commission that the British crown treated the colonies and the colonists as second-class citizens. It was a lesson that he would continue to learn in the future. And although his pride had been injured, he was also learning the art of politics. He would learn to "play the game" with those in authority in order to achieve his goals. He only needed a suitable opening.

Washington's resignation in November 1754 was a short-lived episode, for plans were already in progress for a new campaign against the French. The French and Indian War was now receiving greater attention from England. When George read in the *Virginia Gazette* that the king was sending British regulars under an experienced commander, Major General Edward Braddock, George's pulse throbbed at the idea of serving under a true military man.

GENERAL BRADDOCK COMES TO TOWN

The chance to serve with the elderly, outspoken general was irresistable to George. Feeling confident that he had much to offer and was doing the politic thing, Washington wrote a letter to Braddock, congratulating him on his arrival in America. In March George received a reply, inviting him to meet with Braddock.

George offered his services to Braddock as a volunteer without pay, provided he could attend to personal affairs when not on the campaign. Braddock, aware that George had knowledge of the terrain where the British troops were going, was happy to oblige. Shortly after, he appointed George his aide-de-camp, his confidential assistant. A delighted George wrote his brother John about his good fortune: "I have now a good oportunity, and shall not neglect it, of forming an acquaintance, which may be serviceable hereafter, if I can find it worthwhile pushing my fortune in the military way."

A SECOND TRY AT FORT DUQUESNE

The new plan was to march from Wills Creek, now called Fort Cumberland, to the junction of the Alleghany and Monongahela rivers and capture Fort DuQuesne. Arriving at Frederick, Maryland, General Braddock found what was already a familiar story to Washington—no wagons, horses, and few cattle for the troops' meat supply. When Braddock began to blame the colonials for the shortages, a soft-spoken, rather paunchy gentlemen came to the rescue. His name was Benjamin Franklin.

Though Washington had never met Franklin before, George was impressed with his ability to get things done. In short time, Franklin rounded up 150 wagons and 1,500 horses. He accomplished the task by reminding the Pennsylvania farmers that one of Braddock's officers wore a uniform similar to that of the Hussars, the light cavalry in Europe noted for looting and raiding farms. He warned the residents that if they did not sell willingly at a fair price, a body of soldiers would be sent. The trick worked. The merchandise was delivered on time.

But more than transportation was needed. While waiting for supplies at Fort Cumberland, Washington was shocked to see the inefficiency and the lack of discipline in Braddock's command. Braddock seemed to be good-natured and more than willing to let others take over his work, but his officers seemed uninterested in tackling the job. Drunkenness and gambling were common among the soldiers, and so was their interest in the Indian women encamped nearby.

Washington made it a point of telling Braddock about the kind of warfare practiced by the Indians and the French. He explained that Indians did not line up in formation to shoot, but hid behind bushes and trees to ambush the enemy. Braddock would not hear of changing the traditional military procedures and expressed his contempt for those who fought in such an "ungentlemanly manner."

It seemed as if the campaign would never swing into action. The wagons brought from England were too heavy and wide for the lightweight American horses to handle. Troops were advancing at only two miles a day. When Braddock finally sought some advice, George was more than glad to give it. He told Braddock that the troops needed to move more quickly, ahead of the slow-moving wagons. He suggested that a detachment of 1,200 men with 300 pieces of artillery march ahead of the wagons and carry their provisions on horseback. If the wagons then followed at their own speed, it would still be possible to take Fort DuQuesne before French reinforcements could get there.

Braddock agreed to Washington's plan. But before they could start, George became very ill with fever and sharp pains in his head. When a doctor warned George that moving with the advance party could kill him, he agreed to remain behind after Braddock promised to bring him to the front when the advance party was ready to attack. For days, Washington rode in a wagon moving at a snail's pace, almost too sick to care.

Massacre at Monongahela

When he was finally well enough to travel with one of the wagons moving to the front, George arrived to find the army encamped only 12 miles from Fort DuQuesne. On July 9, 1755, the troops began crossing the Monongahela River. If they could only get to the other side without being attacked by the enemy, the rest of the campaign would be easy! By 2:00 P.M. the crossing had been completed and the advance guard of 1,200 men confidently marched ahead. Braddock was in the lead; beside him was a rather shaky Washington, still recuperating from his illness.

Suddenly there loomed before them what seemed to be a wall of men — the enemy! Before the British grenadiers could attack, the French commander signaled with his arms to the right and to the left. As ear-piercing warwhoops shattered the stillness, French soldiers raced to the woods on either side and began to encircle the British troops. Shots from both flanks echoed in the air. Those in the British lines who did not fall, retreated, straight into the carefully drawn-up lines of their own men. The mounted officers were ideal targets for the invisible enemy. In the confusion, Washington's horse was shot. As it sank under him, George had the presence of mind to leap clear. Then, when a riderless horse raced by, he grabbed the reins and jumped on.

As Braddock and Washington tried to rally the men to regroup and attack, George's horse was again shot out from under him. A bullet also pierced his hat and another gashed his coat. Then Braddock was struck with a charge that splintered his arm and pierced his lung.

The situation was hopeless. In a mad frenzy to run from the scene, frightened, panicky men clogged the river, throwing aside their guns and even their clothing. With two fellow officers, George struggled to bring order to the retreat.

As the sun began to set, the last of the survivors struggled up the east bank of the river and started to march home. In the darkness, Braddock, still alive, was carried on a litter. When the exhausted soldiers could no longer carry him, Braddock was forced to mount his horse.

The Death of Braddock

Braddock died on the night of July 13, a few miles west of the ruins of Fort Necessity. Washington ordered the general to be buried in the middle of the road so that, as they continued their retreat, the wagons would roll over the grave and the soldiers would trample the earth. Thus, no mark of the burial site would remain. The enemy eventually learned of Braddock's death, but they could never find his grave to despoil it.

It was a weak and dispirited Washington who finally returned to the peace of Mount Vernon. The terrible nightmare of the retreat, the groans of the wounded, and his own weakened condition plagued Washington for weeks. Added to this was the humiliation of a second defeat at Fort DuQuesne. In a letter to his brother Augustine, Washington said, "I have been on the losing order ever since I entered the service. . ." Never again would he serve unless he was in charge.

AN IRRESISTIBLE OFFER

Only a month after the death of Braddock, Washington was once again serving in the Virginia militia. With no soldiers to protect the frontier, Indians began attacking helpless pioneer settlers. Once again, Governor Dinwiddie offered George an appointment as colonel and "as commander of all the [Virginia] forces." But when George learned that he would not have the privilege of selecting his own officers, he refused the commission. A compromise was finally reached. The captains had already been named, but Washington could appoint his own field officers.

The new commander, now 23 years old, immediately set to work. He ordered his officers to begin recruiting men as quickly as possible. Because the recruits would be worthless without strict military discipline, Washington also issued orders to all officers to set high expectations of behavior. And he had the new recruits trained for the kind of warfare that might be expected in fighting the Indians.

In October 1755, a dispatch rider brought news that the Indians had surrounded and cut off settlements in the Winchester area. Washington immediately rode to Fort Cumberland, where he was met by Captain John Dagworthy, an officer who had survived the Fort DuQuesne campaign. Dagworthy then proceeded to inform Washington that since he (Dagworthy) had a royal commission, *he* was in command.

Who Is in Charge?

Once more – the issue of command! This time Washington was determined to settle the matter once and for all. When Governor Dinwiddie admitted he could do nothing, George rode north to Boston to appeal to the acting commander-in-chief in America, Governor William Shirley.

The trip gave George his first glimpse of the country north of Virginia and an introduction to many of the leaders of the colonies. In each of the cities passed through, he was entertained by military or society figures, eager to make the acquaintance of the tall commander of the Virginia regiments and the wealthy master of Mount Vernon.

Unfortunately, however, the journey did not solve the problem of George's military commission. Lord Loudon, who succeeded Governor Shirley as the commander-in-chief, made it clear to George that the British had no intention of transforming the Virginia forces into royal regiments. Without that, Washington's hopes of gaining a royal commission were dashed. Even as a colonel, he would always be subordinate to any officer with a royal commission. In a letter to Dinwiddie, George wrote, "We can't conceive that being Americans should deprive us of the benefits of British subjects." It was 1757, and Washington was beginning to think of himself not as an Englishman, or even a Virginian, but as a new breed—an American.

A HOLLOW VICTORY

Returning home, Washington continued to serve as commander of the Virginia militia. It was an impossible task—trying to guard a 400-mile frontier with 700 poorly disciplined men who were ill-fed, poorly clothed, and whose pay was often delayed by order of the legislature in Williamsburg. The effort was beginning to sap Washington's strength. But even a severe illness did not keep him from responding to the call when he was asked to serve again in an expedition to capture Fort DuQuesne.

This time, the campaign was led by a Scotsman, Brigadier General John Forbes. Washington worked hard to convince Forbes that they should once again attack Fort DuQuesne by using the road George had helped Braddock to build. Forbes, however, decided to attack this time through Pennsylvania, rather than over the road that had been used twice before unsuccessfully. The new route would be 40 miles shorter and would avoid the dangerous crossing at the Monongahela River. Although Washington was disappointed when his knowledge and advice were not accepted, he and his troops, nevertheless, followed Forbes west.

On the night of November 24, 1758, Forbes' army was encamped about 12 miles from Fort DuQuesne. Suddenly the stillness of the night was broken by the clatter of hoofbeats. An Indian scout returning from the fort announced that it was in flames. The French had gone! After four years, the prize was theirs for the taking—without battle, or flags of surrender, or booty of any kind.

Despite this hollow victory, what had Washington gained over the four years he had served in the French and Indian War? Although he had never commanded more than 1,000 men, he had learned the need for discipline, the importance of getting supplies on time, and the knowledge that shortages were inevitable and had to be dealt with in any way possible. He had also acquired a reputation for undertaking any assignment, no matter how difficult, and doing it well and carefully. He had even learned how to control both his temper and a stubborn streak. He had proven that he had physical stamina, courage, and unusual maturity and judgment for a man his age. And those, both older and younger, who met and listened to the dignified, self-confident 27-year-old, recognized the signs of a born leader.

Chapter 5
Of Heart and Hearth

Mount Vernon needed a mistress! George loved the serenity of his lovely estate, but weary of war and plagued by illness, he was finding it a lonely place. There was no doubt that Washington enjoyed the company of ladies, but either he had never thought too seriously about marriage or he had been too caught up with his military career to do much about it.

As a 16-year-old, George had thought himself in love with Sally Fairfax, wife of his friend, George William Fairfax. Then, on his trip to Boston in 1757, he had courted Mary Philipse, one of the wealthiest women in New York. Now it was a young widow, Martha Custis, who captured his attention.

Though she came from a modest family, at age 18 Martha had married the heir to a large fortune, Daniel Parke Custis, a man who was 20 years older. Martha, now the mother of two children—Jack, age four, and Patsy, age two—was pretty, tiny (five feet tall), and a woman of good common sense. Her gentle ways seemed to provide just the kind of soothing manner that the exhausted and lonely bachelor needed.

It took just two meetings for George and Martha to decide that marriage would enhance both their lives. On his

*This painting of Martha Washington shows her as a mature
woman, wearing the cap of an 18th-century American lady.*
(Library of Congress.)

first visit to her home, Washington had won over young Jack by giving him a ride on his horse, and he had been duly appreciative of little Patsy's charms. Both actions endeared him to Martha. For a woman who had been married to a much older man, the handsome colonel, so close in age, must have seemed a most attractive mate. For George, the marriage would mean a large addition to his fortune—15,000 acres of land, much of it in valuable lots near Williamsburg, 150 slaves, and "White House," the Custis estate on the York River.

WASHINGTON ENTERS POLITICS

George had no difficulty in adjusting to civilian life. The idea of resigning his commission had probably been on his mind while he was courting Martha during the spring of 1758. At that time, he agreed to run for political office. But because the march to Fort DuQuesne kept him from campaigning personally, his friends agreed to help him out.

Entertaining thirsty voters was commonplace in early American elections. On a steaming hot election day in the summer of 1758, George's friends made sure that the voters did not lack for liquid refreshments. At a cost of 160 gallons of rum, beer, and cider, (about 1½ quarts per voter), he easily won the election. On his 27th birthday, February 22, 1759, George took his seat in the House of Burgesses.

The French and Indian War now seemed very far away. Washington read about the British campaigns in the north in the newspapers and was cheered by the British victories at Ticonderoga and Quebec. In 1760, he applauded the capture of Montreal, which brought final defeat to the French. But George was now deeply immersed in his new life. In a letter to a friend, he wrote, "I am now, I believe, fixed at this seat with an agreeable consort for life, and hope to find more happiness in retirement than I ever experienced amidst a wide and bustling world." And for more than 15 years, that would be true.

MASTER OF MOUNT VERNON

Washington saw the task of overseeing Martha's lands and his own as a challenge, and he applied the same energy and care to this task as he had applied to the problems of military life. He regularly purchased and read books on farming. Because he was disturbed that tobacco and corn were planted year in and year out until the land was exhausted, he became a pioneer in rotating field crops with alfalfa and clover in order to restore the soil. He also experimented in growing wheat, and when he saw that a profit could be made by grinding the wheat into flour, he built a flour mill.

Nor was the master of Mount Vernon an armchair manager. He would roll up his sleeves and help his workers when necessary. He was also quite creative, improving a plow and inventing a farm tool like a seed drill for sowing and covering seeds.

On Slavery

Washington accepted the institution of slavery but hated the slave trade. By 1774 he must have begun to question the system, for he signed a resolution of the House of Burgesses that declared "our earnest wishes to see an entire stop for-

ever to such wicked, cruel and unnatural trade." In his later
years, he favored legislation that would gradually emancipate,
or free, the slaves. In his last will, he ordered that all of his
slaves be set free after Martha's death—and this was done.

George was concerned about the welfare of his slaves.
He saw to it that they were well fed and clothed, and that
they had the services of a doctor. Whenever possible, families were kept together. But he was also strict with those who
did not do their share. On a few occasions, he shipped "mis-
behaving fellows" to the West Indies to be sold.

The Social Whirl

Life at Mount Vernon was not all work. Because plantations
were so distant from one another, individuals or whole families would come to visit for several days or a week and be
well entertained. House parties were frequent, and picnics,
barbecues, and clambakes were regular parts of the Washington hospitality at Mount Vernon.

George was a superb horseman and enjoyed the sport
of fox hunting. Other entertainment at Mount Vernon included
duck hunting as well as billiards and cards with a bit of gambling. In his carefully kept records, Washington often shows
small losses at cards or billiards.

For the winter session of the House of Burgesses, Martha and the children would join George in Williamsburg,
where there were balls, horse racing, and theater. Dancing
was one of George's great pleasures, and he was known to
dance as long as three hours during an evening so as not to
disappoint any of the ladies. It was a diversion that he enjoyed right through the Revolutionary War and during his
presidency. Even at age 64, he was still cutting a smart figure
on the dance floor.

The Washington family, painted by Edward Savage. At the left is Washington's stepson, Jack, and standing next to Martha is his stepdaughter, Patty. (Library of Congress.)

PAPA WASHINGTON

For most people, the image of Washington, at least as portrayed in his paintings, is that of a serious and sedate gentleman. Few can envision him swinging a giggling, teenage stepdaughter through the paces of a dance. Yet he was a loving, caring father to Patsy and Jack, who called him "Papa."

George would beam with delight as he watched the children excitedly open boxes from London—Prussian toy soldiers for Jack and a fashionably dressed baby doll or handsome silver shoes or a silk coat for Patsy. For eight years, he employed a tutor for the children and ordered the many books required for their education. When Patsy was ready for piano lessons, a spinet was shipped from England. Each child had black companions, a few years older than themselves, who served as both playmates and servants.

At age 12, Patsy began having epileptic seizures. Despite care by the best doctors of the time, she died at age 16. In a letter to a friend, the grieving stepfather explained, "After she was seized with one of her usual fits...[she] expired in less than two minutes without uttering a word, a groan or scarce a sigh."

Washington's own disappointment in not having any children of his own, particularly a son, was reflected later in his extension of fatherly friendship to such young men as Alexander Hamilton, the Marquis de Lafayette, and Lafayette's own son. He also showed it in paying college expenses for a friends's son and in other charitable gestures to the children of less fortunate friends.

PATRICK HENRY KINDLES A FLAME

"Boring" was a word Washington might have used to describe most of his time in the Virginia legislature. He took care of his constituents' requests and voted according to his own best judgment. He attended sessions regularly but contributed little to the debates. Unless the subject truly interested him, he tended to sit back and leave the speech-making to others. But in 1765, the situation changed.

England decided that the heavy debts of the French and Indian War should be paid by the American colonists. The money was to be raised by a stamp tax on a list of items ranging from wills and pamphlets to playing cards and dice. The tax varied from one cent on newspapers to the equivalent of

10 dollars on a school diploma. The colonists had been taxed before, but only by the acts of their *own* colonial legislatures.

It took the newest member of the Virginia legislature, a plainly dressed fellow known mainly for his fiddle-playing and story-telling ability, to put into words what many members of the House of Burgesses had been feeling. His name was Patrick Henry. In simple words he drew up a series of resolutions protesting the new tax. When some of the legislators began to bait him, his temper rose. He stood up defiantly and argued that the Stamp Act was an act of tyranny—the work of Parliament and king, not of the people of Virginia. When some members in the audience began to shout, "Treason! Treason!" Henry raised a fist and shouted back, "If this be treason, make the most of it!"

Sparked by Henry's words, the legislators quickly passed the protest resolutions. News of the Virginia resolutions passed quickly through the colonies and ignited fires of protest everywhere. Patrick Henry's words also fanned Washington's growing anger with England. Within the year, the Stamp Act would be repealed (done away with), but the flame of protest that it created continued to glow.

Chapter 6

Immersed in Politics

"**N**o more imports! No more taxes!" This was the cry that raced through the colonies during the summer of 1767. Although the Stamp Act had been repealed, a whole new series of taxes, called the Townshend Acts, had been imposed by the British upon the colonists without their consent. Word of these new taxes stirred the people of the colonies to action. Washington learned that merchants and citizens in other colonies had gotten together and agreed not to import certain goods from England. In May 1969, when George went to Williamsburg for the opening of the new session of the legislature, he had in his pocket a similar plan that he and George Mason, another member of the House of Burgesses, had developed. But before he could present the plan, a series of resolutions were passed on May 16, including one which affirmed that only the House of Burgesses had the right to tax the inhabitants of Virginia.

The next day, the business of the assembly was interrupted by a message from the new governor of Virginia, Baron de Botetourt. The House clerk strode down the aisle and announced, "The governor commands the immediate attendance of your House in the Council Chamber." The Speaker of the House, Peyton Randolph, rose and marched to the chamber, with all of the House members following behind. When all were assembled at the large table before him, the governor rose and declared, "I have heard of your resolves and [predict] ill of their effect. You have made it my duty to dissolve you."

Dissolved! How dare the governor dissolve the legislature! Quickly and quietly, the message was passed along, "Meet in Raleigh Tavern." There, in an act of defiance, the members of the House reconvened to plan their next step. Washington then pulled from his pocket the plan that he and Mason had devised and explained its contents. A motion was then passed to form an association that would include a committee, on which Washington would serve, to put the plan into action. For the first time, Washington was taking a leading role in politics.

In a letter to George Mason that spring, Washington wrote, "It seems highly necessary that something should be done to . . . maintain the liberty which we had derived from our ancestors. . . . No man . . . should hesitate a moment to use arms in defence of so valuable a blessing . . . yet arms . . . should be the last resort."

BACKLASH

Having lost much of their business in the colonies, British merchants pressed Parliament until the Townshend Acts were repealed, except for the tax on tea. The colonists then began a boycott of tea. In 1773, when ships carrying tea reached New York and Philadelphia, they were forced to turn back. But when other ships carrying tea attempted to unload in Boston, a group called the Sons of Liberty planned otherwise. Led by a young radical lawyer named Samuel Adams, the Sons of Liberty, disguised as Indians, boarded the ships and dumped the tea, valued at $75,000 into Boston Harbor. The resulting furor created just the kind of publicity Adams had hoped it would. Parliament retaliated by closing the port of Boston until the town paid for the tea.

Being a man of property, Washington did not approve of the destruction of private property or the actions of the Sons of Liberty. But the action of Parliament disturbed him even more. If one port could be closed by British law or force, then the same could happen to any port in the colonies.

A year earlier, the Virginia legislature had voted to establish a Committee of Correspondence. Its goal was to maintain contact with the other colonies, sharing information of the proceedings of the British Parliament or any other action that would affect the welfare of the colonists. Other colonies soon established similar committees.

Now the Virginians were recommending that the Committee of Correspondence communicate with the other colonies to urge them to send representatives "to meet in general congress . . . to deliberate on those measures which the united interests of America may from time to time require." A truly revolutionary idea! It was a proclamation that the colonies would unite for a common cause and that they had need to meet on a regular basis—an annual congress for *all* the colonies. When elections were held for seven Virginia representatives to the First Continental Congress, Washington was one of the first three chosen.

FIRST CONTINENTAL CONGRESS

Along with fellow delegates Patrick Henry and Edmund Pendleton, Washington arrived in Philadelphia on September 4, 1774, for the first meeting of the Continental Congress. Peyton Randolph, also a member of the Virginia delegation, was chosen speaker. The first question to arise was whether each colony would have one vote or whether the vote was to be based on population. The decision was one vote for each colony.

Because Washington was not immediately selected for any committee, he had time to accept invitations from delegates and hospitable Pennsylvanians who were eager to meet the well-known soldier of the French and Indian War. For Washington, it was an opportunity to meet people from other colonies. He also avidly read the many pamphlets and newspapers published in Philadelphia, thereby increasing his knowledge of the country and the issues facing the Continental Congress.

Among the resolutions passed at the convention was one in support of the Massachusetts Colony. Another was an agreement against the consumption of tea and the importation of British goods and other taxed items. It was also decided that Congress would meet again in May 1775.

Washington's role at the First Continental Congress had been more as an observer than as a participant. Yet others had been impressed with the fact that he was a good listener, asked thoughtful questions, and gave sound advice. For George, the experience had widened his outlook from that of a Virginian to that of an American.

Back home in Virginia, George found that people were beginning to think of preparations for war. At the Virginia convention to select delegates for the Second Continental Congress in 1775, Patrick Henry summed up the new mood. In a ringing speech that has become part of American history, he said, "Is life so dear, or peace so sweet, as to be purchased at the price of chains and slavery? . . . I know not what course others may take, but as for me, give me liberty or give me death!"

THE BATTLE OF LEXINGTON

Washington was preparing for his trip as a delegate to the Second Continental Congress when he received word of bloodshed in Massachusetts. On the morning of April 19, 1775, 700 British regulars were sent to destroy American military supplies in the town of Concord. At the village of Lexington, a volunteer group, called Minute Men, were waiting for the British. When they failed to disperse quickly enough, the British commander ordered his soldiers to open fire, leaving eight Americans dead and 10 wounded.

Reading the news, Washington felt more than ever that his place was in Philadelphia. Yet, plantation business suffered every time he was away from home. He also hated to leave the serenity of Mount Vernon, his family, and his friends.

On the morning of May 4, 1775, all was in readiness for Washington's departure. The jingling of the four horses being hitched to his carriage reminded George that it was time for him to leave. Standing near the doorway, Martha lifted up her hands to George's coat lapels, rose on her tiptoes, and pulled his face down to hers for a farewell kiss. It would not be for long — only a month or two. She could not know that her husband at age 42, was embarking on a journey far beyond her imagination and his.

THE NEW COMMANDER-IN-CHIEF

While traveling through Baltimore on his way to Philadelphia, George was invited to review a company of volunteers. Then, when he reached the outskirts of Philadelphia, a group of 500 military officers on horseback escorted Washington's carriage into town, while bystanders cheered and applauded.

Was all this display of enthusiasm for the military and for Colonel Washington a hint of what was to come?

When the Second Continental Congress convened, there was not the same unanimous approval of measures as at the meeting of the First Congress. This time the issue was war! The feeling was that the colonies would, of course, defend themselves in case of attack, but few wanted to deliberately provoke war. Washington voted for conciliation with the British, but he now had little hope that peaceful gestures would succeed. Why else would he begin to appear at the sessions in the blue uniform he had worn in the French and Indian War? Was he saying that the time had come for combat?

Each of the delegates discussed the plans his colony was making for defense, yet the group proceeded carefully. They talked about authorizing military companies and how to fund them. Boston Harbor was still under blockade and when the Massachusetts delegation called upon the convention to undertake "the regulation and general direction" of the New England army, it was clear that someone would need to take command.

Washington seemed to be the best choice, especially since he was a Virginian. If a New Englander were chosen, it might seem to be a regional problem rather than one affecting all the colonies. John Adams, a rather short and stout gentleman who was the leader of the Massachusetts delegation, rose to offer his candidate.

"I have one person only in mind." Adams paused dramatically for a moment and then went on. "The commander I have in mind is a gentleman from Virginia." Hearing this, Washington, who had been sitting quietly, bolted for the nearest door.

Ignoring Washington's departure, Adams continued, "I refer to one whose skill and experience as an officer, whose independent fortune attest to his good judgment and a man who will be a means of uniting the efforts of the colonies more cordially than will be possible under any other leader — George Washington!"

After a brief debate, Washington was unanimously elected general and commander-in-chief of the Continental forces. Later that day, Washington confided to Patrick Henry, "Remember what I now tell you. From the date I enter upon the command of the American armies, I date my fall and the ruin of my reputation."

Washington had fled at the time of Adams' nomination because he was most uncomfortable with the role of commander-in-chief. He felt he lacked the necessary military experience for such an assignment. (He immediately went out and purchased five books on military matters.) He refused to accept the salary approved by the Congress, stating that he wished to make no profit, merely to cover his expenses.

Never was a man commissioned under such strange circumstances. Washington had been given command of an army which, as yet, did not exist, in a war which had not been declared. Indeed, there was no country to fight for, since the Declaration of Independence would not be written until a year later. Moreover, as the first figure to be given a responsibility for all the colonies, Washington bore a unique position. As one biographer wrote, "Thus, from the first moment of his command, Washington was more than a military leader: he was the eagle, the standard, the flag, the living symbol of the cause."

Yet those at the convention seemed satisfied with their selection. Washington's military bearing and dignity gave him an appearance that made others confident of his ability. And his 16 years of experience as a legislator and master of Mount Vernon had matured him and given him insights that would be useful in dealing with his soldiers — and with the Congress.

The hardest task was writing to Martha. With love and tenderness, George explained to her that he had many misgivings about the task upon which he was about to embark. What neither of them could know was how many years would pass before his return to Mount Vernon.

Chapter 7

War and Independence

How could a war be fought when men enlisted for only one year—men who had no military discipline or training? How could one supply an army when one had to depend upon the legislatures of 13 different colonies to provide funds? How did one oppose the mighty British Navy with colonial merchant ships that had few guns or other armaments? These were among the worries that swirled through Washington's mind as he began his journey from Philadelphia to Boston. He had only gone a day when a rider brought him news of the calamity at Breed's Hill.

THE BATTLE OF BREED'S HILL

The British plan was to occupy Boston, New York, and Philadelphia as a way of sealing off New England from the rest of the colonies. The hills around Boston gave a commanding view of the harbor and offered a perfect place for gun emplacements. The first major battle of the Revolutionary War was fought not on Bunker Hill but on a smaller hill, called Breed's Hill. Here, under the darkness of night on June 17, 1775, a group of rebels had entrenched themselves. Facing them was Thomas Gage, Commander-in-Chief of His Majesty's Forces in America, and three major generals, William Howe, Henry Clinton and John Burgoyne, along with their troops. Four generals for the blockade of Boston, a town of 20,000 people!

Determined to dislodge the rebels from their position, Howe ordered 2,000 men, with bayonets drawn, to ascend Breed's Hill in precise battlefield formation. When the British were within 50 feet of the American trenches, a blast of bullets ripped into the British line. Again and again, the British reorganized and threw new lines of soldiers forward, until the ground was slippery with the blood of fallen men. When the American soldiers' ammunition ran out, they hurled nails as well as scraps of metal and stones at the enemy. At the end, using their muskets to parry the bayonets of the Redcoats, as the British troops were called because of the color of their coats, the remaining patriots fled.

Though Gage had regained the hill, it was hardly a victory. He had lost more than twice as many men, all trained soldiers, against a group of volunteer farm boys. The Americans had demonstrated that a colonial militia could stand up to British regulars and perform with courage and determination. For the British Parliament, news of the battle dashed any hopes of reconciliation. From here on, it was all-out war.

That summer, fall, and winter, Washington was bottled up in Boston, busy trying to turn farm boys into a disciplined army. Things seemed at a stalemate. One ray of sunshine during that dreary winter was the arrival of Martha, along with her son Jack and his wife.

The British Evacuate Boston

One of the young officers who Washington had begun to appreciate was Henry Knox. In the winter of 1775-1776, George sent Knox on a secret assignment—to bring back to Boston

60 cannon from the British fort the Americans had captured at Ticonderoga, New York. It was a tremendous task, requiring sledges to be pulled over steep mountains, deep ravines, and across the frozen Hudson River. The effort paid off!

By March 1, all was in readiness. When the cannons, placed so that they completely encircled Boston, were fired, Howe was taken by surprise. For almost a week, the two sides exchanged fire. Then, on the morning of March 8, Howe sent a messenger to Washington with a flag of truce. Under the terms of surrender, the British evacuated Boston in return for the safe passage of their troops and for those colonists sympathetic to the British cause.

With Boston in American hands, Washington could now begin to move south, with some of the 200 cannon, small arms, and ammunition Howe had left behind.

RETREAT FROM NEW YORK

For his victory in Boston, the Continental Congress voted Washington a medal and Harvard College made him an honorary Doctor of Law. But neither honor could compensate for Washington's new concerns. He knew that Howe's retreat from Boston was only temporary. New York would be the next place where the British would strike. When informed that a fleet of British ships was on its way to New York City, Washington went there with Martha as quickly as possible.

Other news also arrived. On July 2, 1776, 12 colonies at the Second Continental Congress voted for American independence from Great Britain. The official Declaration of Independence was signed on July 4. The last link with England had been broken!

Good news also arrived from South Carolina, where General Charles Lee had succeeded in beating off an attack by General Henry Clinton. But there was bad news from the north. At the request of the Second Continental Congress, General Benedict Arnold had gone to Canada in an attempt to win the French to the American cause and to capture the city of Quebec. Now word had come that Arnold had been wounded, many of his men had died of smallpox, and what was left of his army was in full flight from the British. The frontiers of New England and New York were now open to attack from the north.

For six weeks Washington's men dug mud forts on the small islands in New York's harbor. Then, on August 12 the British fleet of almost 100 ships arrived. As the frightened Americans looked on, an array of troops—kilted Scotsmen, British grenadiers, and hired German soldiers called Hessians—disembarked from the ships. For days, more and more men came ashore on Long Island. Howe waited until all was ready and then, on August 26, he struck.

Sandwiched between British regulars and a Hessian force, Washington's troops on Long Island were cut to pieces. The American forces struggled across the marshy land in retreat. Had Howe pursued them, the largest force of Continental soldiers might have been destroyed. But remembering the loss of his men at Breed's Hill, Howe was not about to risk such an onslaught again. Washington, leading the retreat, was determined to get his soldiers off Long Island and across the East River to Manhattan.

Under the cover of night, 10,000 to 12,000 soldiers and fleeing farmers and their families were ferried across the river. Because men were still struggling ashore when dawn broke, Washington was terrified that the enemy might learn of the night's work before it could be completed. But a misty rain began falling and then a heavy fog rolled in. The fog became so thick that boats and men could not be seen six feet away. Just as the last boats disappeared into the fog, Washington heard shots. The British had learned of the evacuation!

Because he was outnumbered, there was little Washington could do except stay ahead of the enemy, who pursued him into Manhattan and then north to White Plains. By November, Washington's army had fled across the Hudson River to New Jersey and was moving south toward the Pennsylvania side of the Delaware River. As a frigid December descended on the land, the British settled into winter quarters, mostly in New York. But a contingent of 2,000 to 3,000 Hessian soldiers were camped at Trenton, New Jersey, a village directly opposite Washington's position on the Delaware River.

A LOW POINT AND A HIGH POINT

For Washington, December of 1776 seemed a time of utter despair. All through the fall, men had deserted to return to their farms to harvest crops. Militia promised by the various colonies often arrived late. And, as the end of the year approached, the terms of enlistment of many of the men and officers came to an end. It was possible that by January 1 Washington could be left with only 1,200 experienced army men.

Showdown at Trenton

Desperate, Washington had to make a show of strength, and the village of Trenton seemed as good a place as any to attempt a battle. It had only two main streets and was held by a relatively small number of Hessian soldiers. Washington's plan was to send his troops across the Delaware at different points and march to Trenton along different roads to the two main streets in the village. By coming in from two sides, there would be no escape for the enemy. Washington also deliberately chose to attack on Christmas Day, when he hoped that the Hessians would be groggy from too much celebration and would least suspect an attack.

Christmas Eve was very cold and damp, and a storm was brewing. Washington moved his men down to the river bank, where boats were hidden. Under the cover of night, men and artillery were loaded into the boats and ferried across the river. The wind whipped snow, sleet, and rain across the men's faces, and the frigid air stiffened their wet clothes into frozen coats of armor. Ice began to clog the river, and the task seemed to take forever. Washington had hoped the crossing would be completed by midnight, but it was not until 4:00 A.M. that the last boatload of men, horses, and cannon landed on the east shore.

Five miles yet to Trenton. Could they do it? The men had to keep moving; anyone who stopped would surely freeze to death. The horses skidded on the ice and the snow made it almost impossible to see six feet ahead. Light in the east signalled dawn as the men trudged on, white figures in a silent world.

When the American troops finally reached Trenton, it took the Hessian sentries several moments to realize what was happening. By the time they sounded the alert, the Americans had mounted cannons at both ends of the two main streets. Before the bewildered Hessians could form into battlelines, they found themselves facing a blazing artillery fire. When they tried to escape through the surrounding fields, Continental soldiers were waiting for them. The trap was closed!

It did not take long for the Hessians to surrender. When the air had cleared, Hessian wounded and dead lay on the streets. Over 900 enemy soldiers were captured, along with cannon, ammunition, and other valuable supplies. And not a single American life had been lost! In its darkest hour, the Continental Army had won a most important victory.

The Battle of Trenton on Christmas Day, 1776, marked a high point for the Continental Army. The victory over the Hessian soldiers gave new life to the American Revolution. (Library of Congress.)

A Reputation and a Country at Stake

The victory at Trenton could not have come at a better moment, for Washington was about to take a big gamble on his personal reputation. In 48 hours, the enlistment of most of his men would end. Without congressional consent or funding, Washington decided to offer a bounty of ten dollars to those men who would stay on for six more weeks. He then asked his officers to parade their regiments before him.

Seated on a prancing horse, the commander-in-chief spoke to the men. He praised their efforts at Trenton, made his offer, and begged the men not to leave. Then he ordered the drummer to beat the drum for volunteers. Not a man stepped forward! Washington felt personally humiliated, but he would not accept defeat. Wheeling his horse around, he again rode to the center of the line and faced the men. In an affectionate but pleading voice, he began:

> My brave fellows, you have done all I asked you to do and more than could be reasonably expected, but your country is at stake: your wives, your houses and all that you hold dear. . . . The present is emphatically the crisis which is to decide our destiny.

Once more the drummer beat his drum. Washington's heart pounded as he waited. Finally, a soldier nudged his friend, "I will if you will." The two stepped forward — then two more — and more, until nearly all the soldiers advanced to re-enlist. At the end, more than 1,000 men agreed to stay.

The gamble paid off, for a day or two later, the Continental Congress sent word to Washington that, for the next six months, they were giving him almost unlimited powers to conduct the war as he saw fit. For some military men, it would have been an opportunity to forget civilian authority and take over as a dictator. Washington, however, saw it as a tremendous responsibility and assured the Congress:

Instead of thinking myself freed from all civil obligations by
this mark of confidence, I shall constantly bear in mind that
as the sword was the last resort for the preservation of our
liberties, so it ought to be the first to be laid aside when these
liberties are firmly established.

Victory at Princeton

Learning of the American victory at Trenton, General Howe
was furious. How could "three regiments of a people who
make war a profession lay down their arms to a ragged and
undisciplined militia?" He immediately dispatched General
Lord Cornwallis and a large force of British regulars to Princeton, New Jersey. Leaving a small force at Princeton, Cornwallis rushed to catch Washington at Trenton. In sight of
Washington's troops on the other side of the river, Cornwallis
camped out of range of the American artillery.

Realizing that he was vastly outnumbered, Washington,
heady from the victory over the Hessians, gambled once more
on a risky ploy. If he could retreat from the scene before Cornwallis realized it, the American troops could race to Princeton and overwhelm the few British regiments that Cornwallis
had left there. If he failed, however, his army would be trapped
between the British forces.

That night, the Americans kept their fires going and the
soldiers made loud noises as if they were digging trenches.
At midnight, they silently abandoned the camp and began
a wide sweep around the enemy on the opposite shore.

As daylight appeared, the bridge leading to Princeton
came into view. Washington ordered General Hugh Mercer
to destroy the bridge in order to cut off Cornwallis from the
troops at Princeton. But before Mercer's men could complete
their assignment, Redcoats with bayonets drawn advanced on
them.

The Pennsylvania militia was closest to Washington, so he ordered them into the battle. For a few agonizing moments, the Americans milled in confusion. Then Washington galloped among them, shouting, "Parade with us, my brave fellows. There is but a handful of the enemy and we [will] have them directly!"

Two cannons were brought up, but Washington ordered the men not to fire until the command was given. Silently the Americans advanced. When they were within 30 yards of the enemy, Washington galloped to the front and gave the command to open fire.

Washington had never been an armchair general; he was not one to make plans and then leave the soldiering to others. In his earliest battles during the French and Indian War, he had been out front, leading his men into battle. For a man who had voiced doubts about his qualifications as a military leader, once into the fray, Washington seemed to feel invincible. It was as if he felt that nothing could harm him. And once more, at Princeton, the tall, mounted figure raced ahead and urged his men forward.

Washington's aide, Colonel Edward Fitzgerald, could not bear the sight. Situated between the two armies, Washington was a towering target. Fitzgerald covered his face with his hat. It was not until the firing ceased that Fitzgerald dared to look. All around him lay the wounded and dying, but the commander-in-chief still sat astride his white horse — untouched.

The battle had been won. However, Washington barely had time to congratulate his men when word arrived that Cornwallis was advancing. The American troops had just enough time to swap their old blankets for new British ones before making a hasty retreat. The victories at Trenton and Princeton had put new spirit into the Revolution.

Washington's Infamous Teeth

Rumor has it that Gilbert Stuart, painter of one of the most famous portraits of George Washington, did not like him and deliberately drew attention to his mouth in order to highlight his dental problems. Certainly Stuart's most famous portrait, *The Athenaeum* makes Washington look stern and prim, mostly due to the expression around his mouth. In other portraits and the life mask by Jean Antoine Houdon of Paris, Washington's mouth varied from year to year, depending on what set of false teeth he was wearing at the time. For a man of great strength and stamina, Washington's biggest physical problem seems to have been his teeth.

Many stories abound about Washington's teeth. One is that he had a set of wooden teeth. He did not. Another was that Paul Revere, the New England silversmith made him a set of teeth. He never did.

By the time Washington became President, he had only one good tooth left. This eventually loosened and came out. It was given to John Greenwood, a New York dentist, who proudly wore it on his watch chain. In 1789 Greenwood made Washington a set of false teeth out of hippopotamus and elephant tusks. The teeth operated on a set of heavy gold spiral springs, which must have been anything but comfortable. At one point Washington complained that the teeth had turned black. Greenwood explained that it was the result of port wine, which was

Washington's favorite drink. The dentist suggested that Washington clean his teeth with a brush and some finely scraped chalk.

This was not the only correspondence regarding Washington's teeth. As commander-in-chief of the Continental Army and as President, he would constantly seek out the dentist who might make his life more bearable. Even the artist Charles Peale, who painted Washington's portrait in 1772, created a set of teeth for him. In June 1783, Washington learned that a well-known French dentist, Jean Pierre Le Mayeur, had been trying to get through the American lines from New York. Washington immediately contacted the lieutenant colonel in command to give the dentist safe conduct through the lines. Le Mayeur was brought to Washington's headquarters, where whatever was done was managed behind closed doors. Washington later invited Le Mayeur to visit Mount Vernon. The dentist was amazed at the ''civility and attention that His Excellency and Mrs. Washington [paid] to a poor dentist.''

The matter of his teeth—or lack of them—was a source of much embarrassment to Washington. During the Revolutionary War, he was making arrangements for a new set of false teeth when, much to his horror, the correspondence fell into the hands of the British. The British kindly did not make the information public, but it must have caused much laughter among those officers who read the letter.

In order to maintain as much secrecy as possible about his dental problems, Washington even camouflaged a dental bill by paying the dentist's hat bill instead. He urged any member of his staff who might learn such information to maintain complete silence on the subject.

Washington's dental woes had to affect the food he ate, his speech, and his personality. He certainly had to be careful about what was served at public dinners. (He could hardly display discomfort or leave the table to remove his dentures.) He probably had trouble pronouncing long words and "s" sounds. And he had to show caution about laughing too heartily, lest a mouthful of springs be noticed by the public.

For a man much concerned about his reputation, dignity, and image, the dental problems of the first President of the United States must have been a source of much distress.

Chapter 8

Agony, Allies, and Achievement

In January 1777, Washington was camped at Morristown, New Jersey, for the winter, trying to solve the many problems that plagued him. Two arrivals helped his state of mind during that dreary winter. One was his wife, Martha; the second was a new aide-de-camp, Alexander Hamilton. Though only 20 years old, the bright, young officer had already earned a reputation as a writer for the patriotic cause and as a soldier. Born in the West Indies, Hamilton spoke French well, a service Washington would call upon often as time went on.

In August, Washington was sent another 20-year-old aide to whom he would also become much attached, the Marquis de Lafayette. A French aristocrat, Lafayette was made an honorary major general by the Continental Congress, despite the fact that he had not one day of military experience. Washington found the fair-haired Lafayette to be an excellent staff member, eager to learn both English and the military arts. It is interesting to note that both young men, orphaned at an early age, created fatherly feelings in Washington. Lafayette enjoyed Washington's attention; arrogant and proud Hamilton, on the other hand, was to strain the relationship and at times cause the general grave concern.

PROBLEMS AND MORE PROBLEMS

One of Washington's most severe problems was the lack of adequate medical care for his troops. Too many men were dying of typhus, dysentery, or smallpox. Washington worked hard to obtain more sanitary conditions, as well as serum for inoculations against smallpox.

Despite the victories at Trenton and Princeton, enlistments were still a problem. State militias were unreliable, often being drawn away for home service at crucial times. What was called the Continental Army consisted only of 3,000 to 4,000 experienced soldiers. In fact, when an officer once rushed in asking permission to arrest a spy, Washington's reply was, "Don't arrest him. Invite him to dinner and then, as if by accident, drop a hint that the army has 12,000 men." Washington knew that the British would not be fooled for long, but he felt no guilt about reporting to the enemy and to the Congress exaggerated figures about enemy losses and playing down the number of his own.

Washington was sure that Howe's next move would be to take Philadelphia. Capturing the city where the Continental Congress was meeting could bring disorder to the new government. But Howe was playing a cat-and-mouse game, and Washington found it hard to know where to deploy his small forces. Then, in May, word came that General John Burgoyne had been sent by Howe toward Ticonderoga and Saratoga, New York, with 8,000 men. Washington had no alternative but to send a contingent north to assist the American forces there. The man he chose to lead the Continental troops was General Horatio Gates.

However, Washington selected Gates with grave concern because of a rumor that Gates and an Irish-born French colonel, Thomas Conway, were undermining Washington's reputation and hinting that the war would progress far better under a new commander-in-chief. Despite his concern about Gates' loyalty and his dislike of Conway, Washington gave Gates, an able general, the assignment and also sent his best riflemen along. That reduced the number of troops available to Washington to defend Philadelphia.

The waiting game ended on August 31, 1777, when Howe's forces landed on the shores of Chesapeake Bay and began a 60-mile trek inland to Philadelphia. Washington decided to make his stand against Howe at Chadds Ford on Brandywine Creek, north of Wilmington, Delaware. It would turn out to be one of the most inglorious episodes of Washington's career. What occurred at Chadds Ford on September 11 is difficult to understand. As one of Washington's biographers described it, "Washington conducted [the battle] as if he were in a daze."

In addition to being greatly outnumbered by more disciplined British troops, Washington also failed to scout the land well enough. Moreover, the map he used was inadequate. By the time he had evaluated conflicting intelligence reports that he received, the American troops were face to face with the enemy. The Americans were soundly defeated, and Washington could do little but reassemble his forces and retreat. On September 26 Howe marched into Philadelphia, five days after the members of the Continental Congress had fled the city.

To add fuel to the fire of discontent with Washington's leadership, word arrived from the north that Gates had won a decisive victory over Burgoyne at Saratoga. Burgoyne surrendered to Gates on October 17 after being overwhelmed by superior forces that included reinforcements from New England and New York state militia.

The Dissent Dies

The winter of 1777-1778 also saw the end of the secret plot by Thomas Conway, General Gates, and Washington's former aide, Thomas Mifflin, to overthrow Washington as supreme commander of the American forces. After Washington received word that Conway had sent a letter to Gates defaming Washington's character, he said that he would resign if this undermining of his reputation continued. This possibility prompted Henry Laurens, the president of the Continental Congress, to write, "In Washington's ruin would be involved the ruin of our cause." Officers who were fiercely loyal to Washington offered to duel anyone who dared to speak or write slanderous statements about their commander-in-chief. When Conway then offered to resign, Congress, to his surprise, agreed. The secret plot to remove Washington as the leader of the Continental Army had come to an end.

Two lessons were learned from the experience. Washington's officers realized that beneath the general's usually amiable and polite manner was a man who could be an unflinching enemy, especially when it involved his reputation. Congress also learned that men of good judgment all over the country understood and sympathized with the tremendous burden under which Washington bore his command.

Winter at Valley Forge

During the same time, Washington and his men were struggling with the worst winter and the worst physical conditions his army had yet endured. While Howe settled in Philadelphia for the winter, Washington chose Valley Forge, Pennsylvania, as the winter quarters for his men.

Keeping his troops supplied with adequate food and clothing had always been a problem for Washington, but now

Washington inspects the starving and poorly clothed soldiers who endured the terrible winter of 1777–1778 at Valley Forge. (Library of Congress.)

it became critical. Individual states might send supplies to their own militia, but Congress lacked enough funds to supply the entire Continental Army. Food, clothing, blankets, and other supplies were dangerously low. During that winter, some men had only blankets to cover their nakedness; others had no shoes. And all suffered days when there was no food, not even bread.

On many a night, as Washington strolled the camp, he would hear the men chant, "No meat, no meat." By January, the chant had become, "No pay, no clothes, no provisions, no rum." It was not until mid-February that all the men were adequately housed and supplies began to arrive with some regularity.

Despite the hardships, the winter at Valley Forge created a strong bond among the men and officers who endured the ordeal. In earlier encampments, men on short enlistments came and went. Most of the men at Valley Forge, however, were on long-term enlistments, they had experienced warfare, and they had proven their abilities as soldiers. Although they came from many different states, they were beginning to think in terms of a country rather than of their own local regions. They had become comrades who could joke about the terrible hardships. But most important, they had become a seasoned, effective army.

In February, for the first time in many months, Martha was able to join George again. As always, Martha's presence greatly lifted Washington's spirits.

THE FRENCH CONNECTION

For some time, the French had been supplying the Americans with food, arms, and ammunition. Benjamin Franklin, a patriot and statesman much admired by the French, had gone to France in December 1776 and succeeded in gaining promises of assistance. However, the French were not about to incur a new war with their old enemy, England, unless they could be assured that the American Revolution was going to be successful. The Battle of Saratoga was the event that gave the French that confidence and in February 1778, they signed an open alliance with the United States. The French loans and supplies kept the new nation afloat when things seemed at their worst and a fleet, under Comte de Grasse, would prove itself valuable at the Battle of Yorktown.

Another French export was volunteers, but most did not know a word of English and lacked military experience. Washington was grateful to find a few Frenchmen with expertise in cavalry and engineering – skills that most of his generals lacked.

HAMILTON RESIGNS

For four years, Alexander Hamilton had served as Washington's aide. There is no doubt that Washington held him in the highest esteem. "There are few men to be found of his age," he wrote, "who have a more general knowledge than he possesses and none whose soul is more firmly engaged in the cause."

Washington had sent him on some important missions but had never given him the field command for which he had begged. Hamilton had wanted to become Congress' superintendent of finance or to be made a major general – but either Washington needed him at hand or his backing came too late. Now married to an aristocratic New Yorker, daughter of General Philip Schuyler, Hamilton was tired of being dependent on Washington's good graces.

In February 1781, Hamilton kept the commander-in-chief

This portrait of Alexander Hamilton reveals the elegant young man who served Washington during the Revolutionary War and later during his presidency. (Library of Congress.)

waiting for some time. When Washington berated him, Hamilton retorted, "I will hand in my resignation immediately." Washington's first reaction was fury, but he soon realized that the young man could not be expected to serve him forever. He also could sympathize with Hamilton's need to gain independence and personal recognition. Had he not been much the same as a young man? He gave Hamilton a battalion of light infantry and gave him an opportunity to distinguish himself in the most decisive battle of the war, the Battle of Yorktown.

YORKTOWN: THE DECISIVE BATTLE

It was now January 1781. For three years, Washington had been waiting to recapture New York. While holed up for the winter along the Hudson River, events seemed to go from bad to worse. The summer before, Gates had met Cornwallis in South Carolina and the American troops had been severely beaten. The smell of defeat lingered in the air. Weary, hungry, and without pay, groups of soldiers in Pennsylvania and New Jersey began to mutiny. After one mutiny had been put down, Washington ordered the ringleaders to be executed as an example to others.

In 1779 Lafayette had returned to France to plead the American cause. As a result of his efforts, the French sent General Comte de Rochambeau with 5,000 troops and a supply of heavy siege cannon. Admiral Comte de Barras arrived later with a fleet of ships, as did Admiral Comte de Grasse. After consultation with the French officers, Washington now realized that the best place to attack the British was not New York, but Yorktown, Virginia, where Cornwallis had settled with 10,000 men. The plan of attack was based on deception, careful timing, and surprise.

Admiral de Grasse would sail north from the West Indies with 29 warships and 3,000 men. De Barras, with the siege guns, would come south from Rhode Island, sailing around the British fleet in New York Harbor. Rochambeau would march south from Rhode Island, skirt the British troops in New York, and join Washington at Trenton for the march south to the top of Chesapeake Bay. Troops would then be transported by water to Yorktown.

The Ruse Works

Word was deliberately spread in the New York area that the Americans were looking for boats and pontoons to make bridges, hoping the British would believe Washington was planning an attack there. The plan worked. Washington began marching south on August 19, but it was not until August 31 that British intelligence discovered the strategy and the British fleet set sail for Chesapeake Bay. Washington was concerned that the British were planning to attack de Barras. He was also worried because no word had been received about de Grasse's fleet. The timing of the operation had to be perfect or all would be lost. Meanwhile, the French and American forces had joined up and had swept through Philadelphia.

On September 5 Washington received good news. De Grasse was in Chesapeake Bay with 28 ships and 3,000 troops. On September 8 the French fleet attacked the British ships, damaging them so badly that the British were forced to limp back to New York. Washington normally accepted all news calmly, but this time he could hardly contain his excitement. For six years he had worked towards this moment, and now all was in readiness.

While his troops continued to march south, Washington rode ahead so he could spend a few days at Mount Vernon. How could he not go home when he was so close? Washington had not seen his beloved home for six years and four months. Waiting to greet him were Martha and four little step-grandchildren he had never met before. After a few restful days at Mount Vernon, he rejoined his troops.

The Noose Tightens

By September 28 the trap was ready to be closed. Washington's men were now within a mile of the enemy's camp at Yorktown. Artillery had been delivered by de Barras while the British Navy was engaged with de Grasse. Trenches were built opposite the main British defenses. For three days the British kept up a steady fire, but Washington was not about to waste his ammunition until he had guns close enough to storm the British defenses with a minimum of bloodshed.

The siege continued as more French troops were brought up. Finally the time came to storm the enemy's walls. Among those assigned the dangerous task of attacking the British batteries were Lafayette and Hamilton. On the night of October 14, their troops moved forward silently with fixed bayonets. Quickly the Americans clambered over the barriers the British had set up. Musket fire filled the air. Then Washington heard his men shout and cheer. The British positions had been captured.

Victory and Peace

Cornwallis was now in a desperate position. The only escape was by ship, but his troops were turned back by a sudden storm. The end of the siege came on October 17, when a British messenger arrived under a white flag of truce carrying a letter from Cornwallis. The official surrender was signed on October 19, 1781.

For all practical purposes, the victory at Yorktown ended the Revolutionary War. When the news of Cornwallis' surrender reached England, the British realized that continued efforts to hold the colonies were useless. John Adams and Benjamin Franklin then negotiated the formal treaty that ended the war. Called the Treaty of Paris, it was signed in Paris, France, in September 1783. By the provisions of the document, the United States not only gained its independence, it was also granted all lands from the Atlantic Ocean to the Mississippi River.

WASHINGTON IS OFFERED A CROWN

Before the peace treaty was signed, however, the goals of the American Revolution were threatened by the prospect of another mutiny by its long-suffering soldiers. Because many officers believed that they would never receive their back pay, rumors abounded that the army was going to force the Continental Congress to dissolve and make Washington king.

In the spring of 1782, Lewis Nicola, one of Washington's colonels, sent a letter to Washington suggesting that he accept the title of George the First of the United States and set up a monarchy. Washington immediately sent back a letter stating, "You could not have found a person to whom your schemes are more disagreeable."

But the issue would not die. Within months, another desperate situation arose. The states had refused to let Congress collect taxes on imported and exported goods. Congress needed this tax money to pay the officers and men who had served so valiantly in the war. A group of officers then circulated a letter stating that they refused to disband until the states took action to provide money for Congress. Washington received a copy of the letter, which urged all officers to come to a special meeting in Newburgh, New York.

*At his headquarters at Newburgh, New York, Washington
managed to talk rebellious soldiers out of a possible military
takeover of the new country.* (Library of Congress.)

Though Washington knew the men were right in their
demands, he could not agree to the action they were planning, which could lead to a military takeover of the government. All that the country had been fighting for during the
past seven years could be lost. Washington knew he could
not let the meeting take place without trying to convince the
men of the danger of their actions.

On the day of the meeting, Washington strode to the
crude platform that had been set up. Carefully, he explained
that Congress was aware of the services the men had per-
formed and that, given time, Congress would act justly. The
men sat and listened, sullen and unmoved by Washington's

words. Desperate for support, he then pulled out a letter from a member of Congress to show the officers what the legislature was trying to do.

A Fumble Saves the Day

Suddenly the men realized that something was wrong. Washington was stumbling over his words; he seemed unable to read the letter. Reaching into his pocket, he pulled out something only his closest friends had seen him use — a pair of glasses. With a sad and weary voice, Washington explained, "Gentlemen, you will permit me to put on my spectacles, for I have not only grown gray but almost blind in the service of my country."

The simple but dramatic words tugged at the hearts of the men as their eyes filled with tears. After Washington left the hall, the officers voted to express confidence in the justice of Congress. Thomas Jefferson was later to write of that day, "The moderation of a single character probably prevented this Revolution from being closed, as most others have been, by a subversion of that liberty it was intended to establish."

By his refusal to encourage a military takeover, Washington had preserved the republic.

Chapter 9

Retirement and Recall

C hristmas Eve 1783. The sound of hoofbeats echoed in the cold Virginia air long before the rider galloped into view. Washington was home! After almost nine years, he was home—home for Christmas—home for good.

Washington bid farewell to his officers at Fraunces' Tavern in New York on December 4, a few days after the British had formally evacuated the city. On December 23, he offered his official resignation as commander-in-chief to Congress, which was then meeting at Annapolis, Maryland. As at Fraunces' Tavern, his words brought tears to those whose afffection he had earned during the many years of war. He concluded the brief three-minute speech by saying, "I here offer my commission and take my leave of all the employ-ments of public life." Washington may have resigned from the army for a second time, but he was far from through with public life.

George had much work to do at Mount Vernon. He found the plantation deeply in debt. Slaves had been sold to pay for taxes, and his nephew, who had taken care of the estate during his absence, had taken no pay for five years. He also found himself playing the role of national host to many people from abroad who vied to meet the great general. Though Washington enjoyed his guests, the cost of entertaining them added greatly to his living expenses. There was also a great deal of correspondence, letters from people he knew in the country and overseas, which took much of his time and energy. In 1786, Washington hired a young Harvard graduate, Tobias Lear, as his private secretary. Lear became another of Washington's devoted "sons," serving him through his presidency and until his death.

Washington was also delighted to unofficially adopt two of Martha's grandchildren. Jack Custis had died toward the end of the war and his wife had remarried. The two older children had remained with their mother and stepfather. But four-year-old Nellie and George Washington Parke Custis, not quite three, had come to live at Mount Vernon.

THE POTOMAC CANAL PROJECT

Even before the war, George had high hopes for the settlement of the land west of the Appalachian Mountains. As a young man, he had dreamed of connecting the many waterways in that area so that commerce and trade would link the Ohio River to the East Coast. (It would also greatly enhance the value of his own western properties.)

George had been home only a short time when Thomas Jefferson, a Virginia congressman and author of the Declaration of Independence, wrote him that unless something was done on the project very soon, the state of New York would monopolize the western trade. That state had already begun to build a canal along the Mohawk and Hudson rivers. This news was just the push Washington needed.

For the next few years, George became passionately involved in organizing and drawing up plans for the Potomac Canal Company. In putting together the project, he had to gain the cooperation of the two states which bordered the rivers, Virginia and Maryland. Soon other states were drawn in, until it was decided to invite all of the states to a conference at Annapolis.

For some time, Washington had felt the need for more cooperation between all the states. Having suffered during the revolution with problems resulting from local pride and concerns, he knew that the idea of a truly national state of mind needed to be encouraged if the United States was to survive.

Although Washington did not attend the meeting at Annapolis, the results were all that he had hoped for. The delegates there had called for a general convention to be held in Philadelphia in May 1987 to "render the constitution of the federal government adequate to the exigencies [needs] of the Union." The time had come to look at the common problems all the states were facing and begin to deal with them.

CHAOS IN THE NEW COUNTRY

The first efforts toward national unity, the Articles of Confederation had taken years to ratify and had proven inadequate for running the country during the war because among other things, Congress lacked the power to collect taxes. Washington recognized this in his last official letter to the states, a document that came to be known as "Washington's legacy." In it, he called for "a convention of the people" to establish "a federal constitution" and "an indissoluble union."

James Madison, a fellow Virginian, later to be the fourth President of the United States, worked with Washington to design and pass the Constitution. (Library of Congress.)

In addition, he urged the establishment of an adequate army and navy, "a sacred regard for public justice" (payment of what was owed to soldiers and civilians), and forgetting "local prejudice" which divided the nation. Now others were beginning to come around to Washington's point of view.

Rebellion!

By 1786 the country was suffering from inflation — money was losing value and goods were more expensive. In Massachusetts, in what came to be known as Shays' Rebellion, farmers rioted in protest against taxes they were unable to pay. Something had to be done to unify the nation and bring order out of the economic and political chaos with which the new country was struggling.

When Virginia drew up its list of delegates to the convention in Philadelphia, Washington's name headed the list. Before leaving for Philadelphia, Washington met at Mount Vernon with James Madison, a brilliant man of 38 who was also a Virginia delegate to the convention. Together they discussed ideas to create a strong federal or centralized government.

Once again, Washington worried about his reputation. He and Benjamin Franklin would be the two most prominent men at the convention. What would happen if he were put in a position of political leadership and failed? For Washington, decision-making had always been a slow and painfully thought out process. Sometimes the process was accompanied by real pains from rheumatism or other ailments. But once a decision was made, the pains would disappear and he would energetically set to the task at hand.

THE CONSTITUTIONAL CONVENTION

The task at hand was later to be known as the Constitutional Convention. Though scheduled to begin on May 14, 1787, the opening session was delayed for two weeks because of bad weather and bad roads. The time was not wasted, however, for members of the Virginia delegation met daily to take the ideas conceived by Washington and Madison at Mount Vernon and create a well-organized plan for strengthening the national government. The Virginia Plan, as it was named, called for three branches of government—legislative, executive, and judicial—with a two-house legislature.

How would the delegates receive this plan? This was no rewriting or patching of the Articles of Confederation. Rather, it was a totally new and radical concept. Would the states be willing to give up some of their powers in order to create a strong central government? At meeting after meeting, Washington gently but persuasively began to convince the delegates to take the vigorous stand that was needed. But some were not sure that the people were ready for such a great change.

Gouverneur Morris, a Pennsylvania delegate, remembered Washington saying, "It is too probable that no plan we propose will be adopted. Perhaps another conflict is to be sustained. If, to please the people, we offer what we ourselves disapprove, how can we afterwards defend our work?" Washington also knew that even if a constitution could be agreed upon, it would require much education to get the people to ratify (approve) it.

President of the Convention

Washington, as expected, was unanimously elected as president of the Constitutional Convention. On the floor he did little, but behind the scenes he worked hard to promote the

This portrait of Washington was painted by the noted American artist, Charles Willson Peale, at the time of the Constitutional Convention. It was designed as a tribute by Peale to his former commander and to show his approval of the convention itself. (Library of Congress.)

Federalist view. (Those opposed to this view were known as Antifederalists.) May rolled into June and then July. The biggest roadblock seemed to be the idea of representation in Congress according to population. Because the small states opposed the large ones on this issue, the convention seemed doomed. Franklin then offered "The Great Compromise." In the House, representation would be based on population; in the Senate, every state, regardless of size, would have two members. The compromise was accepted.

The issue that personally affected Washington most was how the executive branch, the presidency, would be run. Some delegates favored a committee of three; others (including Washington) favored a single strong executive, which was the view that was finally adopted.

On September 17, 1787, the Constitution was signed, after which it was submitted to Congress and then to all the states for ratification. On June 21, 1788, after nine states had ratified the document, Congress was able to set a date for the election of a President and the organization of the new government. By that time it was obvious that Washington was going to be the unanimous choice of the electors for the presidency.

Accepting the presidency, however, presented a difficult decision for Washington. During his years away from Mount Vernon, the wealth of his estate had so greatly declined that by the winter of 1787-1788, he was seriously in debt and forced to borrow money. It was only when he learned that the President would be paid a regular salary that Washington agreed to serve.

ANOTHER FAREWELL TO MOUNT VERNON

On April 16, 1789, two days after receiving official notice of his unanimous election as the first President of the United States, Washington was on his way to New York, the nation's temporary capital. Martha, Nellie, and little George would join him later. Martha was not happy at the prospect of leaving their home any more than George was. He, at least, had the excitement of starting a grand new experiment, the like of which had never been tried before.

Washington did stop at Fredericksburg to see his mother, who was dying. Till the end, she remained a difficult, complaining woman. Never had she complimented her oldest child on his accomplishments as commander-in-chief of the Continental Army. And no record exists that she praised him on his new role as the first President of the United States.

Chapter 10

His Most Benign Highness

The week between Washington's arrival in New York and his inauguration, was one of small and large decisions. One such decision was determining what the official title of the new national executive should be. John Adams, Washington's Vice-President favored "His Most Benign Highness," while a Senate group favored "His Highness, the President of the United States of America and Protector of the Rights of the Same." Washington, however, wanted no part of such aristocratic foolishness. It was his friend, James Madison, who finally convinced Congress to settle for "the President of the United States."

INAUGURATION DAY

The morning of April 30, 1789, was heralded by the roar of 13 cannons. Promptly at 12:30 P.M., as church bells pealed, Washington was escorted by a committee of Congress to Federal Hall. The inauguration ceremony, which was held on a large porch overlooking Wall and Broad streets, was simple and dignified. As Washington placed his right hand on the

On his route north to his inauguration as President, Washing-
ton was given an elaborate reception by the people of Trenton,
New Jersey. This engraving depicts Washington under an arch
of greenery and a banner that reads, "The hero who defended
the mothers will protect the daughters." (Library of Congress.)

Bible held for him, Robert Livingston, the Chancellor of the
State of New York, asked, "Do you solemnly swear that you
will execute the office of President of the United States and
will, to the best of your ability, preserve, protect, and defend
the Constitution of the United States?"

Washington replied, "I solemnly swear," repeated the
oath, and then added, "So help me God." Then he bent forward and kissed the Bible.

The crowd roared their approval. Then Washington

Washington taking his oath of office as first President of the United States on the balcony of Federal Hall in New York City. (Library of Congress.)

proceeded into the Senate chamber to read his inaugural address, which took less than 20 minutes. Probably the most important aspect of the address was his confirmation of the need for the amendments which Congress would later pass as the Bill of Rights.

Even before the inauguration, Washington realized that finding time to do his job would be his biggest problem. The "open door" policy he had used at Mount Vernon would not work in the capital. So many people came to "see the President" and to seek political appointments that it was almost impossible to conduct his business. Yet if he did not extend invitations and meet the public, he would be acting like a king. He finally decided on two receptions a week, with morning hours set aside for meetings.

The First Lady Arrives

By the end of May, Martha arrived with the two grandchildren. Her presence took much of the social burden from George's shoulders. But Martha, too, found her hours crowded with people and details. She became friends with many of the Congressmen's wives and saw that they were entertained at teas. John Adams' wife Abigail, was a favorite visitor at the presidential mansion on Cherry Street. Their friendship helped smooth some of the jealousy that Adams felt toward the President.

Martha was also vital to Washington's welfare. Shortly after her arrival, George became extremely ill with an infection of the thigh, and twice during his years in office, he had serious bouts with pneumonia, one of which almost proved fatal. It was Martha's constant attention to George's needs that helped see him through these illnesses.

THE FIRST 17 MONTHS

In his reply to the letter notifying him of his election, Washington had written, "I . . . feel my inability to perform [the arduous task], I wish there might not be reason for regretting the choice." Whether it was modesty or his usual concern that his hard-earned reputation not suffer, Washington had reason to worry about undertaking the presidency.

Unlike many of the politicians he worked with, Washington lacked an extensive formal education. He had little knowledge of political history or of the law. On the positive side, however, he had learned to handle people with tact and diplomacy. He also could recognize important ideas while giving careful attention to details. He would need all these talents as he began to work with his Cabinet and the new government.

The first 17 months in office marked a solid record of achievement. Washington put together the new government by organizing departments and by making appointments to the executive and judicial branches—all of which was accomplished with relatively minor grumbling. The last two states, Rhode Island and North Carolina, ratified the Constitution, the Bill of Rights was passed, and Congress supported all of Washington's plans and most of those of his department heads. While all this was going on, Washington was careful to keep the line drawn between what the role of the legislature was and what the role of the President was.

He also put together a first-rate Cabinet. John Jay, who had been secretary of foreign affairs under the Confederation, stayed on until Thomas Jefferson returned from France and could take over as secretary of state. Henry Knox became secretary of war, and Alexander Hamilton was appointed secretary of the treasury. Though not a department head at that time, the attorney general, Edmund Randolph, became a member of the presidential Cabinet. Each man had considerable experience and was well suited for his job. Though Cabinet members did not always agree, there was not any real friction between them. Public sentiment was also with Washington and the new government.

History, Heroes, and Myths

In 1789, when Washington became the first President of the United States, a new nation sprang into being almost before it had time to acquire a history. It needed what all nations need—a history, heroes, and myths.

The United States quickly embraced those Europeans who had explored the country, men like Christopher Columbus, Ponce de Leon, Marquette and Joliet, and Henry Hudson. Their exploits and the background of the country's French, Spanish, and English colonial roots became the foundations of the first history texts printed in the new nation.

Society also has a compelling need to make heroes out of ordinary men, especially in times of crisis. A new nation, particularly, needs an individual who will hold a government together until the people learn to be loyal to the government itself. When George Washington died, one countryman voiced this idea: "[Under Washington] we had one common mind—one common head—one common heart—we were united—we were safe." In the United States, George Washington became the first genuine American hero.

In 1775, even before the United States was declared a nation, Washington became a national hero when he succeeded in forcing the British to evacuate Boston. Books, children, ships, and colleges were named after him. Copies of his portrait hung in homes throughout the land. Coins were minted with his face imprinted on them. When he became

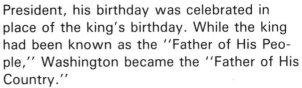

President, his birthday was celebrated in place of the king's birthday. While the king had been known as the "Father of His People," Washington became the "Father of His Country."

Such men as John Adams and James Monroe helped to create the myth by exploiting Washington for his usefulness. They were pleased to have him preside at the Constitutional Convention, and they praised him for his support of the Constitution, knowing his support would ensure ratification by the states.

But no one did a better job of myth creation than Mason Locke Weems, better known as "Parson Weems." Though he was an ordained minister, he served only briefly in the pulpit. After 1793, he put his natural talent for words into writing and selling books. During Washington's second term of office, Weems began contacting publishers about writing books about the President. He once told a publisher, "There's money to be made in Washington's bones," and there was—for Mason Locke Weems.

Even before the President's death, Weems was busy concocting stories heralding the virtues of his hero. Because there was so little documented information about the early years of Washington's life, Weems could invent any "facts" he wanted, since they were virtually impossible to disprove. Yet Weems, according to a note in Washington's diary, met the President only once. The diary, written in the fall of 1787, states, "The Reverend Mr. Weems and a young Dr. Craik, who came here yesterday, left . . . about noon." Washington hardly noticed or talked to the 28-year-old clergyman.

Weems' tales about Washington's youth became part of the folklore of the nation. His story about Washington's cutting down the cherry tree, was recited in schools all over the country. For over a hundred years, the myths of Parson Weems were reprinted in children's books and public school readers. What Weems did was give the middle class 19th-century public what they wanted—a hero with all the middle class virtues.

In time, such myths were "debunked" by historians, who could find no facts to support them. But they remain part of the folklore of the nation. They served their purpose, for they helped to develop a national spirit and inspire patriotism. In Washington's time, they served a much more important purpose. The myths—and the man—helped to unify the new nation.

On November 26, 1790, at the request of Congress, Washington proclaimed a day of Thanksgiving, giving the nation its first national holiday after Independence Day. In December Washington presented his first annual message to Congress, giving an honest and open review of the first 17 months of the new nation. The heart of the message concerned the need for more public education. He saw education as a means of teaching the people "to know and value their own rights . . . to distinguish between oppression and the necessary exercise of lawful authority."

WASHINGTON SPEAKS OUT ON BIGOTRY

In the fall of 1789, Washington decided to make a tour of the northeastern states. He hoped it would give him an understanding of how the people were responding to the new government. The trip accomplished that goal. It also gave the people an opportunity to see their new President and helped to strengthen their support of the Constitution and the nation. In 1791, Washington made a similar trip through the southern states.

In between these journeys, the President made a special trip to Rhode Island because that state had not yet ratified the Constitution prior to his tour of the northeastern states. One of the most noteworthy speeches ever made by Washington was to the members of the Jewish Congregation of Newport:

> It is now no more that toleration is spoken of, as if it was by the indulgence of one class of people, that another enjoyed the exercise of their inherent natural rights. For happily the government of the United States, which gives to bigotry no sanction, to persecution no assistance, requires only that they who live under its protection should demean [conduct] themselves as good citizens, in giving it on all occasions their . . . support.

PLANS FOR A NEW CAPITAL

At a time when news took days or weeks to travel, those who lived closest to the seat of government were at an advantage. One of the earliest issues debated in Congress was where the country's permanent capital should be. Farmers were opposed to placing it in financial centers like New York or Philadelphia. Southerners were concerned about the influence of the Quakers in Pennsylvania, who were beginning to petition for the abolition of slavery. Northerners were equally fearful about southern influence. The decision was a compromise, one that Washington favored strongly, though he did not try to influence Congress.

Philadelphia would be the temporary capital for 10 years, giving the nation time to build a permanent capital on the banks of the Potomac River, less than 15 minutes from Mount Vernon. The precise location was left to Washington to decide. For a man who began his career as surveyor, Washington was excited about the project and threw himself wholeheartedly into it.

While on vacation at Mount Vernon, Washington took time to select the exact site. Not only did he choose the site, he also selected the city planner/architect, Major Pierre Charles L'Enfant. L'Enfant had been one of the first French soldiers to join Washington and, after the war, had earned quite a reputation as an architect in New York. L'Enfant was eager for the assignment for never before had any nation been given the opportunity of deliberately deciding on the location and design of its capital city. Moreover, L'Enfant and Washington saw eye to eye in their vision of the city. It was to be on such a scale that it would leave room for greater development as the nation prospered in the future. For Washington, the new capital became an overwhelming interest.

Washington also chose the best site in the city for the President's house, making sure that the view would be a splendid one. On that spot, the White House stands today. All those involved in the project, Jefferson and Madison among others, agreed that the city should be named Washington and that

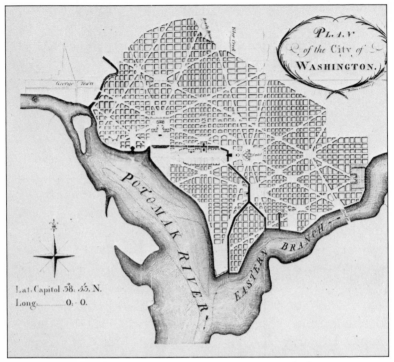

Pierre L'Enfant's plan for the new capital, Washington, D.C.
The Capitol building is at the center, with streets radiating out
in all directions. (Library of Congress.)

the entire 10-square-mile area be called the District of Columbia.

The Capitol building itself, for which Washington laid the cornerstone, was inspired by the Pantheon, a classical French building in Paris. Though the streets were only mud lanes and cows grazed on the Capitol grounds, Washington, D.C., became the official seat of government in 1800. However, it would take another 100 years before the city would achieve the beauty and glory that Washington and L'Enfant had envisioned for it.

A Capital Move

In the fall of 1790, the capital was moved from New York to Philadelphia. The city had rented the finest home available for Washington's residence. He immediately gave orders for additions to the mansion that would make it more suitable for his family. By the winter social season, all was in readiness.

Martha hosted a First Lady's Christmas Eve entertainment. There was also a New Year's Day reception and, in February, a celebration of the President's birthday. These became annual events for the Washington adminstration.

All seemed to be going so well. Yet seeds of disagreement were beginning to take root below the surface. They would burst forth before the end of Washington's first term of office.

Chapter 11

The Road to Political Parties

"**M**r. President, you cannot do it!" Washington listened intently as James Madison gave his opinion. For all those who felt that Hamilton was Washington's most-favored advisor, it was Madison who Washington had turned to for advice about his retirement.

Long before his first term was over, Washington had been making plans to retire. The strain of office, several bouts with illness, and the feeling that he had achieved his goal of keeping the fragile union together made him hungry for the peace and serenity of Mount Vernon. Early in 1792, Washington had made his plans known to Jefferson, Hamilton, Knox, and Madison. Now he was turning to Madison for help in finding the proper time and place for making his retirement public.

"The country cannot risk your retirement now," continued Madison. "It is true that when I urged you to take the presidency I also said that you should retire to private life as soon as possible so that you would not be accused of being overly ambitious."

"But," argued Washington, "from the very beginning I have found myself deficient in many of the essential qualifications. I am inexperienced in public business and unfit to judge legal and Constitutional questions. And now, at age 60, my health worsens—perhaps, my faculties also. I find the situation scarcely tolerable. Besides I sense a spirit of factions in the government," Washington continued. "Though none of the public attacks have been aimed at me directly, I sense I am an indirect object. My presence is not encouraging harmony."

"No matter how difficult the business might have been," responded Madison, "your judgment has been as competent as anyone's could be. Your services are *essential* in uniting all the government. You must stay on until public opinion, the character of the government and the course of the administration should be better decided. Besides who else would make a better candidate? Adams? Jay? Jefferson? Sir, you must make one more sacrifice in order to preserve what you have begun."

Hamilton and Jefferson were urging the same thing. It seemed to be about the only thing the two men seemed to agree upon those days. Jefferson summed up his reasons, "North and South will hang together if they have you to hang on. [Any other person] will be thought [nothing] more than the head of a party."

HAMILTON VERSUS JEFFERSON

A large part of Washington's growing discontent with the presidency was based on the struggle for power between Hamilton and Jefferson. It was not a matter of temperaments that caused the rift; it was, rather, a matter of genuine differences of beliefs.

The first issue that threatened the new nation was a financial one. The financial credit of the United States had to be established. Hamilton, as secretary of the treasury, had pressed for the federal government to assume responsibility for the war debts of all the states. A congressional bill, called the Assumption Bill, also promised to pay the money owed on certificates given to soldiers instead of pay. Unfortunately, most soldiers, unaware of what was going on in the government and needing ready cash, had sold their certificates to speculators.

Hamilton sought support for his bill from Jefferson, but Jefferson was not happy that so many soldiers, having already sold their certificates, would be losing money rightfully due them. Yet, he knew that the war debts had to be taken over in order to establish the national credit. Jefferson agreed to get southern support for the Assumption Bill *if* Hamilton would get northern support for the establishment of the permanent capital along the Potomac River. A deal was struck and the problem was solved.

But the attitude of compromise did not last long. There were too many differences between the two men. Hamilton, a New Yorker, represented the financial interests of the North. He believed that the hope of the nation lay in developing its manufacturing and trade. Jefferson, a southern planter, saw the nation profiting through agriculture and the export of farm products.

Hamilton was a Federalist. He believed in a strong central government, led by a strong executive. He also leaned toward an aristocracy. (At the Constitutional Convention, he had even proposed that the executive be elected for life and, like a king, have the right to veto all legislation at will.) Hamilton further believed in a loose construction of the Constitution—finding interpretations that would benefit the banking and manufacturing interests of the North.

Jefferson, on the other hand, believed in a democratic society where an educated common man would help to elect

Thomas Jefferson served as secretary of state in Washington's Cabinet and later became third President of the United States. (Library of Congress.)

the leaders. He was concerned that too much power might be given to the executive branch of the government. He favored strict adherence to the principles and words of the Constitution. He also believed that those rights not given to the federal government by the Constitution belonged to the states. Jefferson was beginning to think of himself as an Antifederalist, as a Republican.

To Run or Not to Run

What was happening was a split in government—the formation of two political factions—and Washington was caught in the middle. He appealed to both Hamilton and Jefferson for moderation and compromise, but the effort failed. It was as Washington feared. There were now two political parties: the Federalists, represented by Hamilton, and the Republicans, headed by Jefferson. (The Republicans would later call themselves Democratic Republicans and would eventually become the Democratic Party.)

Washington never publicly stated his desire to retire from the presidency, nor did he ever publicly agree to run for a second term. His silence, however, was taken as consent. When the electors, consisting of representatives from each state, met in February 1793, Washington was unanimously re-elected. For Washington, who really had wanted to retire and return to Mount Vernon, the patriot had won over the planter. But his second inauguration could hardly have been a joyous occasion for him. The fact that his inaugural speech was only two sentences long may have indicated something about his feelings.

BAD NEWS ON ALL FRONTS

Personal tragedy added to Washington's sense of depression. George Augustine Washington, his favorite nephew and the family member he had trusted to manage his estate, had died of tuberculosis. The second tragic news came from France. The French Revolution, which had erupted in 1789, also affected Washington personally. His spiritual son, Lafayette, had barely escaped a Paris mob and had fled France, only to be captured and thrown into an Austrian prison. Washington could not help Lafayette without endangering his neutral role as President, but he could help Lafayette's wife. Through a mutual friend, Washington sent funds to assist her.

The French Revolution had initially been greeted with great enthusiasm in the United States. The French Declaration of the Rights of Man and the Citizen owed much to America's Declaration of Independence and its Constitution. Lafayette and a group of moderates seemed to be in control. The news that the French king, Louis XVI, and his wife, Marie Antoinette, had been imprisoned brought cheering Americans out into the streets. Americans also began wearing "Liberty Caps" and calling each other "Citizen" and "Citizeness" instead of Mr. and Mrs. For the pro-French Jefferson, it created a natural opposition party to the aristocratic-loving Hamilton and the Federalists.

Yet, as the French Revolution began to fall apart, many Americans began to worry about the state of chaos in France. Then word was received that France had declared war on England, Holland, and Russia. With these great naval powers now at war, American shipping would certainly be affected. American shipowners might be tempted to set up their ships as privateers, operating independently of the government to support France and attack British vessels.

"Should we actively support France or remain neutral?" That was the question facing Washington's Cabinet. After much debate, a Proclamation of Neutrality was issued in April 1793 stating that the conduct of the United States toward the powers at war would be "friendly and impartial." It warned Americans not to help either side or they would lose the protection of their government.

The Genet Affair

The Proclamation of Neutrality was tested almost immediately with the arrival in Charleston, South Carolina, of Citizen Edmond Genet, minister from France. Genet convinced several shipowners in Charleston to commission their ships as privateers. He then went to Philadelphia, where he was received by Washington and entertained socially by Americans who remembered how France had helped the United States in its struggle against England during the Revolutionary War.

Before long, there was far more serious news about Genet's attempts to obtain American support for the French cause and undo the neutrality proclamation. He had arranged the taking of a British merchant ship, the *Little Sarah*, renamed it the *Petit Democrat* (*Little Democrat*), and outfitted it as a warship. Ordered by the American government to disarm the ship, Genet not only refused but threatened to go over the head of Washington and appeal to the people directly. Then, despite an assurance to Jefferson that the *Petit Democrat* would not sail, it slipped out of port and disappeared. Even Jefferson was now thoroughly upset by the arrogance of Genet.

Disgusted with Genet's behavior, Washington was about to order him back to France when the group in the French government that had appointed Genet was ousted from power. Fearful for his life if he were returned to France, Genet appealed to Washington for permission to remain in the United States. Washington agreed. Genet later married the daughter of Governor Clinton of New York and spent the remainder of his life in that state.

RESIGNATIONS!

The fall of 1793 was a particularly difficult time for Washington. Yellow fever struck the capital, causing families, congressmen, and businessmen to flee the city. Then, Jefferson announced his resignation as secretary of state. Washington reminded Jefferson that in situations where a compromise was not the answer and a decision had to be made, he had favored Jefferson more times than Hamilton. But there was nothing that Washington could do to convince Jefferson to stay on.

A year later, Secretary of the Treasury Hamilton and Secretary of War Knox also resigned. Both men needed to attend to their private business affairs, which, like Washington's, had suffered during their terms of office.

During this trying period, Washington had been giving much thought to another national need — higher education. He now suggested that a national university be established where "young men from all parts of the United States" could study "the different branches of literature, arts and sciences" and also "get fixed in the principles of the Constitution, understand the laws and the true interests and policy of their country." In his will, Washington left shares of stock that he owned in the Potomac Canal Company for such a school, which was eventually established as Washington and Lee University.

THE WHISKEY REBELLION

One of the ways used by the new government to raise revenue was a tax on whiskey, most of which was brewed by Scotch and Irish immigrants on the Pennsylvania frontier. Because the whiskey tax was viewed as a burden by the western farmers, they openly refused to pay it. They even attacked revenue officers and raised a military force to defy the federal government.

Washington recognized that such an open rebellion was a serious threat to national law and order. Therefore, he sent a force of 16,000 federal troops to the frontier in 1794. Faced with overwhelming odds, the "whiskey boys" fled, but two of the leaders were caught and found guilty of treason. How-

ever, because the rebellion had been crushed without the loss
of life, Washington was merciful and pardoned both men. By
his actions, he demonstrated that the new nation could and
would support its federal laws.

PROBLEMS WITH INDIANS

In the Treaty of Paris, England agreed to give to the United
States the British forts that followed the main fur trade routes
along the Great Lakes. They also granted a huge area of fur-
producing wilderness south of the Great Lakes and west of
the Ohio River. But when the time came to turn over the forts
and land, the British refused. In addition, the British were
supplying the Indians in that territory with guns, thereby
preventing Americans from settling across the Ohio River.

To take possession of the forts and land, and to subdue
the Indians, Washington realized that a strong show of military force was needed. In August 1794, General Anthony
Wayne was sent out to the western frontier in Ohio with a
large force. He defeated the Indians and pursued them to Fort
Miami, a British fur post. A year later, the United States
signed a peace treaty, the Treaty of Greenville, with four Ohio
tribes.

When Washington delivered his final annual message to
Congress, he was able to present a positive report on Indian
affairs. He hoped that a new era was beginning for the Indians with "peace with each other and with the United States."
In fact, during one week in November 1796, the President
and Mrs. Washington entertained several Indian chiefs and
their wives at a formal dinner. When the Indian chiefs left
Philadelphia, Washington presented each of them with a dress
coat, rifle, saddle, and a bridle.

The President Sets Precedents

"Few can realize the difficult and delicate part which a man in my position has to act . . . I walk on untrodden ground. There is scarcely any part of my conduct which may not hereafter be drawn into precedent." By these words Washington showed that he recognized the difficult task the first President faced.

What is it like to take an office no one has ever occupied before? What must it be like to know that every act, personal or public, may become a "precedent"—an example for future generations of leaders to follow? That was Washington's predicament when he was elected President.

Beginning in 1792, Washington started a practice that would be followed by all succeeding Presidents. He originally sought advice from his department heads by meeting individually with the secretaries of state, treasury, or war, as particular information was needed. As his department heads began to disagree or come into conflict on issues more and more, Washington decided to bring them together for open dialogue, to hear all sides at one sitting.

The secretaries would arrive at a meeting with written opinions on the items to be discussed. Though the system did not achieve the kind of ready compromise and good will that Washington had hoped, the routine of regular Cabinet meetings became a precedent followed by later Presidents.

The Constitution made the Vice-President, John Adams, presiding officer of the Senate, which was the only responsibility assigned to the Vice-President by that document. Washington might have considered using the Vice-President as his second in command, much as the British king used the prime minister as his chief advisor. But Washington was not particularly fond of Adams. While Adams was serving in the Continental Congress during the Revolutionary War, he had given Washington much trouble. Nor was Adams in any hurry to give advice to the President, fearing he would be blamed if things went wrong. By the end of Washington's first term, the role of Vice-President had become defined as a very secondary one, lacking any particular responsibilities, and remains so even today.

The matter of how the "advise and consent" clause of the Constitution was to be carried out was also open to interpretation. Should there be meetings between the President and the Senate for approval of treaties and appointments or should it be done through correspondence? Washington's initial impulse was to meet with the Senate. When the first opportunity arose for the process to be tried, it proved to be as much a comedy as government business.

One day, Washington arrived at the Senate chamber to discuss a treaty with the Creek Indians. Adams, as presiding officer, arose to read the proposed item, but the rumble and clatter of carriages passing by in the street outside made it almost impossible to hear what Adams was saying. Someone suggested that the windows be closed, after which Adams read the document again. Then a senator asked that a certain section of the treaty be read again. This led to more requests for the re-reading of other sections.

Time passed. Both the temperature and tempers in the room began to rise. As the issue became more confusing, Washington's temper also began to increase. When he could stand the debate no longer, he rose to his feet and shouted, "This defeats every purpose of my coming here."

After his temper cooled, Washington agreed to a postponement of a decision. But when he reappeared, the debate dragged on again, hour after hour. Washington finally obtained acceptance of the treaty, but when he left the Senate, he was heard to say he would "be damned if he ever went there again." He never did. Nor did any of his successors. Treaties and appointments requiring consent are sent to the Senate, debated there, and the results reported to the President.

At least three other decisions by Washington set precedents. Though the Jay Treaty was approved by the Senate, the Republicans in the House were unhappy about its approval. They then voted to force Washington to send them all correspondence on the treaty he had in his files. Washington was stunned.

First, the House had no right to approve or disapprove treaties; the Constitution had assigned that privilege to the Senate. Second, for the House to demand papers intended for the President was stepping on the rights of the executive branch of the government.

Washington's response was definite. He intended to see that the defined responsibilities of each of the three branches of government, as stated in the Constitution, would be preserved. He refused to send the files.

When he put down the Whiskey Rebellion in 1794, Washington set a precedent for using military force to enforce federal laws. In 1962, when John F. Kennedy wanted to ensure that a black, James Meredith, would enter the University of Mississippi, he knew he had the right to call out troops to enforce the federal law, thanks to the precedent set by Washington almost 170 years earlier.

Washington's decision not to serve as President for a third term was accepted as tradition by all Presidents who followed him except one—Franklin Delano Roosevelt. World War II had already been declared in Europe when the 1940 elections rolled around. Roosevelt was elected for an unprecedented third term because the country did not want to change Presidents at such a critical time. For the same reason, in 1944, with the United States still actively involved in the war, Roosevelt was elected for a fourth term, though he was in poor health.

In 1951, the 22nd Amendment to the

Constitution was passed, limiting the President to only eight years in office. The country had decided that the precedent started by Washington was important enough to finally be made official.

Washington had both the privilege and the responsibility of deciding many "firsts." The nation recognized this when, at the time of his death, a member of Congress, Henry Lee, defined Washington as "a citizen, first in war, first in peace, and first in the hearts of his countrymen."

A WEB OF FOREIGN AFFAIRS

American settlers were not only pushing westward, they were also pushing south into territory still held by the Spanish in what are today the states of Florida and Louisiana. Drawn by their mutual fear of the French Revolution, Spain and England had signed an alliance. Washington now worried about what would happen if the British decided to move south from Canada and the Spanish north from Louisiana and Florida.

There were also more problems with England. Under a new set of British regulations, England would not let neutral countries trade with the French West Indies or send arms or food to France. This hurt American trade. Moreover, the British seized hundreds of American ships and confiscated their goods. In 1794 Congress ordered that trade with England be cut off and began making preparations for a possible war. Washington was determined, however, to find a peaceful way, if possible, to settle the situation. In April 1794 he sent John Jay to London as "envoy extraordinary" to negotiate a treaty with England. After all, who could do better in such matters than the man who had been the first Secretary of Foreign Affairs under the Confederation, who had negotiated the Treaty of Paris with England, and who was now Chief Justice of the Supreme Court?

The Jay Treaty

When Jay's treaty finally arrived from London in March 1795, Washington found it less than favorable. Britain did agree to evacuate the western fur posts and forts by June of the following year. Ports in England and in the British West Indies would be open to America, and there would be some payment for the losses of American shipowners. However, Britain did not promise to halt the practice of stopping American ships and taking goods from them. This meant that profitable American products, such as molasses, sugar, and cotton, could not be shipped to France or its possessions without risking seizure by British ships.

The Republicans seized upon the treaty in a massive outpouring of rage. British flags were burned, Jay's effigy was set ablaze in towns all over the country, and Hamilton was stoned in a public debate as he attempted to support the treaty. Any agreement with England would have angered the pro-French supporters, but the continued prospect of American ships being stopped and valuable cargo taken also enraged farmers and merchants.

After much debate, the Senate approved the treaty. Now it was up to Washington. If he used his veto power, it would infuriate the pro-British Federalists, and the spector of war would rise again. If he approved, there would be peace with the greatest naval power of the time. Washington chose peace; he did not veto the treaty.

GOOD NEWS FOR A CHANGE

Washington was delighted to finally receive good news from abroad. Thomas Pinckney, the American ambassador to London, had been sent on a special mission to Spain, which, by 1795, had allied itself with France against Great Britain. Because the Jay Treaty seemed to favor England, Spain began to worry that there might be a secret clause in it by which Britain would aid the United States in an attack on New Orleans and Florida.

Pinckney's efforts were successful beyond all expectations. He negotiated a treaty with Spain which, for the first time, gave the United States unrestricted use of the Mississippi River from its source down to the ocean. Americans were also granted the right to deposit goods for export in New Orleans, where they could then be shipped abroad. The southwest boundary between the United States and Spain was defined at what is today the northern border of Florida. Moreover, Spain pledged to restrain the Indians from violating the new Spanish-United States border.

The Pinckney Treaty was enthusiastically approved by all factions in the Senate and helped to smooth over some of the discontent with the Jay Treaty.

Chapter 12
A Final Peace

The most famous piece of writing attributed to Washington is his Farewell Address. Yet it was never publicly delivered as a speech, was dated six months before he left office, and the writing itself is in Hamilton's writing style. How did that happen?

Early in 1796, Washington began making preparations to leave office by writing a draft of his farewell speech. He asked Hamilton to review the paper, and Hamilton wrote a new draft based on Washington's ideas. The President was very pleased with Hamilton's efforts, which is why the final draft is in Hamilton's literary style. The themes of the address, however, were based on Washington's beliefs about government and what he felt was right for the country.

The Farewell Address was never meant to be delivered publicly. It was a way of informing the public and the legislators that he would not be seeking a third term, thereby opening the door for other candidates seeking the presidency. The completed document is dated September 17, 1796, the day on which Washington had the address delivered to a newspaper, the *American Daily Advertiser*, for publication. As soon as it was printed, it was copied in newspapers all over the country, giving it as much coverage as possible in an age without radio and television.

Though disappointed by some of the events of his second term—the split of the nation into political parties, the resignations of men he knew and trusted, like Hamilton and Jefferson, the Whiskey Rebellion, and the national furor over Jay's Treaty—Washington's address displayed neither anger nor hostility. Rather, it dealt with his hopes for the nation, and offered some cautions and some suggestions. He reminded the people that the nation had begun with "a common cause," independence and liberty, and achieved through common efforts. His first hope was that the country remain unified, that local interests not override national concerns.

He warned the nation to "avoid the necessity of those overgrown military establishments, which under any government . . . are hostile to . . . liberty." He expressed his concern about the development of political parties, particularly along geographical lines, for they "agitate the community and kindle the animosity [hatred] of one part against another." He did admit that, within limits, political parties were useful checks upon the administration of the government and served to keep alive the spirit of liberty.

Washington conveyed his interest in education by urging the nation to promote institutions for the general spread of knowledge in order that public opinion should be enlightened.

Perhaps his greatest contribution was his repetition of the theme of the Proclamation of Neutrality: "Observe good faith and justice toward all nations. Cultivate peace and harmony with all. . . . Steer clear of permanent alliances with any portion of the foreign world." Yet Washington, ever the practical man, made a clear distinction between commercial and political treaties. He believed in extending *commercial* relations (trade) with foreign nations, but to make as few *political* alliances as possible.

Those sections dealing with foreign relations are probably the best remembered, for they served (with minor breaches) as the cornerstone of American foreign policy for more than a hundred years.

THE PAIN AND PLEASURE OF FAREWELL

The last days of Washington's presidency were tinged with pain and pleasure. On his last birthday as President, Philadelphia awoke to a day of festivities, beginning with the ringing of bells and the firing of cannon. In the evening, a ball was held in his honor at Rickett's Amphitheatre. It is said that more than 12,000 people managed to squeeze in to pay their respects to the President and Mrs. Washington. Martha was moved to tears by these strong proofs of public regard. The President never looked better or in finer spirits, and he tried hard to conceal his emotions. But at times, he could scarcely speak.

The inauguration of John Adams, the new President, was held on March 4, 1797, at Congress Hall. Dressed in a handsome black suit with a military hat, Washington marched alone to the hall. John Adams, usually somberly dressed, arrived in a pearl-colored suit, with a sword at his side and a beribboned hat. Following the ceremonies, Adams was to write to his wife his impressions of the day, "The General['s] . . . countenance was as serene and unclouded as the day. He seemed to me to enjoy a triumph over me. Methought I heard him say, 'Ay! I am fairly out and you fairly in. See which of us will be happiest!' "

HOME TO MOUNT VERNON

Washington had so longed for his retirement; he had more than earned it. He might complain about the failings of age, but his mind and body were still active. On days when the weather prevented his daily rounds of Mount Vernon, he would impatiently pace the porch that fronted his home.

Nor would the country let him retire to a peaceful old age. James Monroe, appointed as Washington's last ambassador to France, wrote a book called *A View of the Conduct of the Executive of the United States*. In it, Monroe charged Washington with treachery, of having a pro-British attitude, and not supporting French liberty. Then a letter, written by the new Vice-President, Thomas Jefferson, accused the general of corruption and leanings toward a monarchy. The charges, though unfounded, had to affect a man who had always been very concerned about his reputation. Now, even after his retirement, the Republicans continued to use his reputation for their own ends.

The new President, John Adams, was having his own problems. He suffered much from comparison with Washington. No matter what he did, Adams saw himself in the shadow of the first President. When France threatened war with the United States, Adams was forced to call upon the one man who could unify the country. In 1798 he asked Washington to serve as commander-in-chief and assemble a new army. Reluctantly, Washington accepted the assignment. But it was almost like his first days in service during the French and Indian War. Adams had agreed to let Washington select his own officers, but the usual bickering over rank and command made Washington happy to drop the project when the French war scare ended.

Loving, Lasting Memories

Yet, there were some lovely moments to remember that last year of 1799. His beautiful granddaughter, Nelly Custis, fell in love with a new guest at Mount Vernon, George's nephew, Lawrence Lewis. She chose "Grandpapa's birthday" for her wedding day. The delighted general, still able to fit into his old blue and buff Continental uniform that he had put aside 10 years before, presented quite a handsome figure on the great day. And in November, a great-granddaughter was born at Mount Vernon.

"Tis Well"

By December 1799, Washington was, as usual, making his plans for Mount Vernon for the coming year. On the 12th, he took his daily ride, despite the fact that it had begun to snow around noontime. Returning home, he insisted that there was no reason to change out of his wet clothes, that his great-coat had kept him dry, and he would not hold up dinner any longer. But during the night he began to suffer with a sore throat and labored breathing. For two days Martha and his faithful secretary, Tobias Lear, sat with him while the doctor tried everything he could to cure the general. But by the 14th, Washington knew this would be his last illness. With great clarity of mind, he gave Lear and Martha final instructions about everything from his will to the opening of the burial vault. Sometime before midnight, Washington took his own pulse and whispered his last words, "Tis well."

Martha, at the foot of the bed, looked at Lear. "Is he gone?" Lear nodded, unable to speak. Martha, unconsciously echoed George's words, "Tis well."

THE LEGACY

George Washington's life spanned the most critical years of the birth of the United States. He played a role in every phase — from the protests against English tyranny to the first stirrings of independence, through the Revolution to the first perilous years of the new nation.

He grew from an ambitious, arrogant, barely educated young man, seeking land, money, and personal glory, to a man who could bridle his temper, worry about his inadequacy for the monumental tasks expected of him, and sacrifice his personal fortune for the needs of a nation.

As President, he showed his ability to recognize and encourage the talents of the brilliant young men who came before him—men like Hamilton, Jefferson, Madison, and Lafayette. He learned to work with tight-fisted legislators, temperamental generals, and strongly opinionated Cabinet members. And most important, he maintained the highest standards of behavior and strict attention to what was ethical and morally right. He gave to the new nation a model for the presidency for future generations to follow.

And if any doubted Washington's sincerity in turning down the opportunities for power and glory, as either military man or monarch, one only has to see where he is buried. In a small, secluded, grassy dell overlooking the Potomac River at Mount Vernon, a simple burial vault marks the final resting place for Martha and George Washington.

Bibliography

Andrist, Ralph K., editor. *George Washington: A Biography in His Own Words.* Vol. 1. New York: Newsweek, 1972. Illustrated with paintings and excerpts from Washington's diaries, this book gives a quick overview of the first President's experiences, without interpretation of events or personalities.

Emery, Noemie. *Washington: A Biography.* New York: G. P. Putnam's Sons, 1976. This book offers a fresh approach to Washington's times, his personality, and the Revolution. Besides giving a British view of the Revolution, it analyzes Washington's relationship with the famous men with whom he worked — Hamilton, Jefferson, and Adams, among others.

Fleming, Thomas J. *First in Their Hearts; A Biography of George Washington.* New York: W. W. Norton, 1968. Good junior high level reading, with enough anecdotes about spies and romance to keep the reader interested.

Flexner, James Thomas. *George Washington: The Forge of Experience (1732–1775).* Boston: Little, Brown, 1965. This first of four volumes gives not only fine details about Washington's life, it also interprets the man and the era in which he lived. The other volumes are *George Washington in the American Revolution (1775–1783), George Washington and the New Nation (1783–1793),* and *George Washington: Anguish and Farewell (1793–1799).*

Harwell, Richard. *Washington.* New York: Charles Scribner's Sons, 1968. An excellent abridgement containing more than 700 pages of the seven-volume work by Douglas Freeman entitled *George Washington.* Unless the student needs great depth in understanding a particular period or event in Washington's life, this book is preferred.

Judson, Clara Ingram. *George Washington: Leader of the People.* Chicago: Follett, 1951. An old but well-written dramatized biography of Washington.

McGowan, Tom. *George Washington.* New York: Franklin Watts, 1986. This 60-page book gives a capsule-size version of Washington's life. It has good illustrations.

Morris, Richard B. *Seven Who Shaped Our Destiny: The Founding Fathers as Revolutionaries.* New York: Harper and Row, 1973. The second chapter, entitled "George Washington: Surrogate Father to a Revolutionary Generation," is a first-rate summary of Washington's importance to the American Revolution.

North, Sterling. *George Washington, Frontier Colonel.* New York: Franklin Watts, 1986. This book uses excerpts from Washington's diaries to cover his military career. It ends as Washington embarks on the presidency.

Schwartz, Barry. *George Washington: The Making of an American Symbol.* New York: The Free Press, 1987. This book takes an unusual approach to the subject of Washington. The author explains how Washington played a unique role, becoming the symbol around which the new nation rallied.

Sognnaes, Reidar F. "America's Most Famous Teeth," an article in *Smithsonian Magazine,* February 1973. For those who wish to debunk the myths about Washington's wooden teeth, this bit of research and the illustrations ought to give you all the answers.

Thane, Elswyth. *Washington's Lady.* New York: Dodd, Mead, 1960. Written almost as a novel, with imaginative research, this history of Washington from his wife's point of view is delightful and easy reading. It chronicles Martha's life from her initial impression of the young man who came to court her until his death.

Index

2482